THE
INFINITE
PATIENCE
OF
TIME

THE
INFINITE
PATIENCE
OF
TIME

The story of a Colombian American artist

who stumbled into ALS

BY PATRICIA RIASCOS

SMALL BATCH BOOKS

Amherst, Massachusetts

Library of Congress Control Number: 2019934194
ISBN: 978-1-937650-96-4

SMALL
BATCH
BOOKS

493 SOUTH PLEASANT STREET
AMHERST, MASSACHUSETTS 01002
413.230.3943
SMALLBATCHBOOKS.COM

To my mother, Betty,
who inspired me to aim as high as possible—always—
and whose wise words have guided me through life.

I also want to express my gratitude to Trisha Thompson,
my editor at Small Batch Books, and Lisa Vega, this book's designer.
I am not a writer and, given that English is my second language, it took great patience and
effort to allow the flavor of my prose to show through. Lisa, too, took great care to make sure
that the style of the book complemented my art to the smallest detail.

CONTENTS

THE INFINITE PATIENCE OF TIME

*The story of a Colombian American artist
who stumbled into ALS*

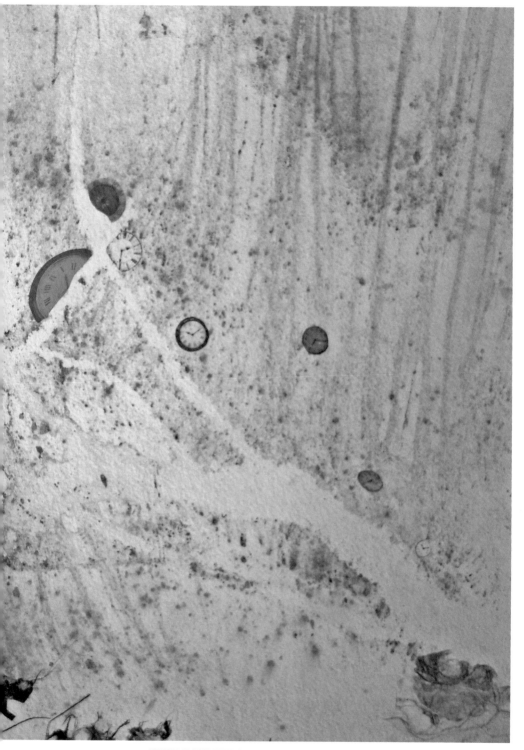

"THE INFINITE PATIENCE OF TIME" (MIXED MEDIA/COLLAGE)

POLICE ENCOUNTERS

JANUARY 2017

Perhaps the feeling that I was being squished emotionally over the last few months prompted me to react the way I did today when a police officer stopped me for an expired car registration.

I should mention that last year, I changed my address with the DMV, and for some reason they keep sending my registration to my old address. In addition, it never arrives on my birthday the way it does for most people. I understand that it is my responsibility to renew my car registration, but car matters are the last thing on my mind these days.

Here was Officer Plank standing at my window, explaining the reasons for the ticket and telling me that he is forty-four years old and no one has to remind *him* that his car needs a new registration. He presented the freaking ticket, and I was fine until then. But then he proceeded to tell me that I needed to fill out this paper on the back, and in about a month I would be getting my appointment for my day in court!

Then I lost it.

"Why do I have to go to court?" I asked him, as a river of tears kept running without my permission. I explained that it is hard enough for me to walk these days, and now if I had to start making trips to the court offices . . . I've never had to go to court before! I was not going, I told him. I couldn't understand why. But he insisted on this.

He started to explain, and I kept getting more and more upset, and it became hard to speak with clarity. He was determined that I would go to court, and I was convinced that I could make him change his mind. After a few minutes of back-and-forth—I on the losing end—I decided I had to give up or I'd run the risk of getting arrested for arguing with a police officer.

He didn't accept my promise that I would get the problem fixed as soon as possible. I even asked him for his email address so I could send him proof, but he didn't think that was a good idea. (I knew it was a long shot.)

I understand that tickets are given mostly for a reason and usually are the driver's fault; however, I felt deep inside that it was the DMV's fault this time. But the officer wouldn't buy it.

In the time span of about one year, I got *almost* three tickets. The first one was for speeding (only about the third one in my lifetime). I had to take an online course and was reminded of the dangers of speeding. I was grateful that I didn't cause any harm to anyone and promised myself I'd do better.

The second is the one I received from Officer Plank.

Then a few days later my sister Vicky came to visit from Nicaragua and I took her for a ride around town. Since tickets and police cars were on my mind due to recent events, I was very mindful of my speed—and also paranoid and looking in my rearview mirror constantly.

When I saw the police car behind me, I thought to myself, *I am so glad I am being careful with my speed. Who knows who is he going after.* I thought he was in a hurry to pass me . . . and then I saw the flickering lights behind me.

This can't be happening! I thought . . . along with some (mental) swearing.

I pulled over, and the officer told me I was speeding. I told him very politely that he was wrong—that I was being very careful not to go over the speed limit because I had just gotten a ticket a few days ago. He insisted, and I did too. I could hear my sister quietly telling me not to argue with the police, and my husband, who was in the back, was thinking the same thing as well, I'm sure.

I showed the officer all of my paperwork, in total compliance since I had just paid the overdue registration. He went to his car, then came back with my papers and mumbled something to the effect of "Go on your way and be careful with your speed."

"But what about the ticket?" I asked. "Where is it?"

"There is no ticket," he said.

And we parted ways . . . but not before I told him how sweet he was. He sounded exasperated and annoyed after hearing me call him that. . . .

I am still wondering what really happened. Was I right? Did he feel sorry? What on earth made him change his mind? That will remain an unsolved mystery.

ETHER

One of the clearest memories I have from early childhood is the smell of ether.

The dictionary describes it as a pleasant-smelling, colorless, volatile liquid. For me, it is one the nastiest odors ever!

I remember very clearly screaming loudly into a mask on my face for my mom to come and get me. I must have been less than four years old.

Many years ago, using a mask to deliver ether as a means of anesthesia before surgery was the method of choice, so I went through this experience several times as a child for my initial hip surgeries.

Patients were required to spend the night in the hospital before a morning procedure, which was sheer torture for me—and, consequently, for my poor mom. I cried the entire night, knowing exactly what would happen the next day. Very early in the morning, the loose and creaking wheels of the stretcher coming to get me was the scariest of sounds. I would beg the nurses to let me stay with my mom. I didn't know why they wanted to "harm" me in such a way.

I don't remember being offered an explanation about why they had to do this. Was I too young to understand the concepts that would help me deal with what surgery is, why it's necessary . . .

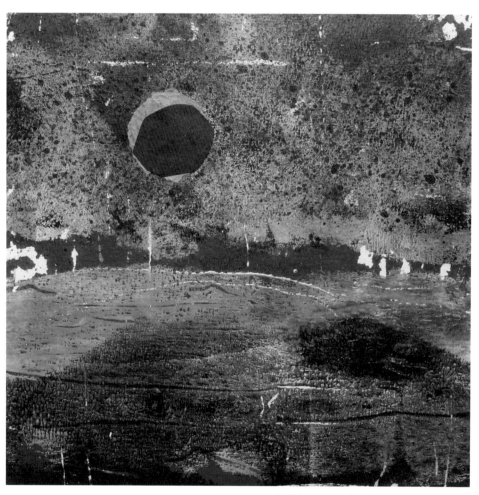

"NIGHT" (MONOTYPE/COLLAGE)

or how much better it would be after everything was over? Now, as an adult, I want an explanation for everything. I question every procedure and every diagnosis. It's not foolproof, but it has helped over the years in many ways.

3   TECHNICAL MALFUNCTIONS

If we were made in a factory, then each of us would come with an instruction manual. I imagine there would be a list of things that each of us would need—"badges" we would need to earn—that would be carefully placed on top of our tiny chests as the conveyer belt went around.

I must have been a model made in a hurry, by someone who needed to go on break or was working on the night shift way too late. My list of badges to "earn" was a long one, and I feel like my body has been malfunctioning ever since I can remember.

I was born with what is called hip dysplasia (when the ball and socket don't fit together properly) in both sides. It's a rare condition that so far has no explanation, although there are several known contributing factors.

I went through several surgeries as a child to correct this, and back then, that meant spending many weeks at the hospital.

My dad had died in an automobile accident when my mother was pregnant with me, and I can only imagine how difficult it was for a new mother to have to deal with all of the logistics. She lived alone and worked as an executive secretary until I was five years old, when she married a wonderful man, a veterinarian well loved by all who knew him. We then moved from Bogotá to the town where he lived, in the beautiful coffee region of Colombia.

By the time I was twelve, I was finished with my hip-related surgeries, including a broken femur that needed to be redone after it had healed. I don't remember exactly how many surgeries there were, but it was probably more than six judging from all the scars.

When we see children with extreme health problems, we feel so sorry for them and can only wonder how miserable they are. You might be surprised, however. For the child, it is their normal. Children don't complain about bad luck; they go with the flow. Children can give us all lessons in courage and acceptance. My only tantrums were on the days before the surgeries took place.

Adolescence is the time to become self-conscious, a time when anything different from what is considered normal is mortifying. Something as mundane as a scar becomes the source of shame—at least it did for me. I felt embarrassed, as my scars were especially long and visible.

My parents decided that it would be a good idea for me to have plastic surgery, since my scars led to keloids, which is excess scar tissue that is dark purple and fibrous and expands in all directions. I ended up needing five plastic surgeries.

During my time as an exchange student in Illinois, I had an accident going through a door that connected the kitchen to the garage, which was four stairs down. The door screen had been taken out to be cleaned, so when I went to push it open, I went through it instead, the back of my knee "brushing" on the way a sharp piece of metal from the grill nearby and acquiring a two-inch laceration that required stitches. That was another scar that needed to be fixed.

By the time I was thirty years old, I had been walking with hip pain for a while. At thirty-nine I had my first hip replacement. By 2015, I had had four hip-replacement surgeries. In between those, I

"IN REPAIR" (ACRYLIC ON CANVAS)

also had a hammertoe fixed and had arthroscopy on my left shoulder, both of which had very painful recoveries. The hip surgeries had lengthy recoveries, but I never felt much pain after the first few days following the surgery.

I feel that I have now earned all my badges, and I'm starting to recognize that I have come full circle, as I will explain.

FULBRIGHT

In college I studied microbiology ("bacteriology" in Colombia). As I was getting ready to graduate, I applied for a Fulbright scholarship to get a master's degree in the United States.

After extensive paperwork, I received the call announcing that I had been awarded the scholarship. I still remember the feeling of achievement, even if it was premature. I felt as if I could almost touch a dream I had had since childhood: I was going to do something special with my life. I wanted to excel in the field that I had chosen.

The last step before leaving was a meeting in Bogotá for the more than one hundred students from all over the country who would be going to the States for graduate studies.

A few weeks before we were supposed to leave, I received a call saying they were having difficulties finding the exact program that I had chosen. I wanted to study food chemistry, but those in charge didn't find anything related to this. I didn't know myself if there was a special name for that particular field. This was the first I was hearing of this issue, and unfortunately, there was no one I could ask questions to, no adviser to help me find a related field I could explore.

So I was left behind, "to apply some other time."

That's how easy an amazing opportunity for free higher education in the States came to an end.

5 BACK TO THE STATES

I still had an urge that I can't really explain to get back to the States.

I had my career and a good job, and I lived comfortably with my parents, enjoying a rewarding relationship with them—particularly with my mother, given the special link we had after those difficult first years of my life.

I worked for a couple of years until I had collected about $1,500 U.S. dollars. (This was almost forty years ago—still not a lot of money, but I considered it decent enough for the trip.)

In 1980, at age twenty-five, I finally was on a plane to California. Claudia, my good friend from college (whom I'm still in close contact with), lived in Huntington Beach and offered to pick me up at the airport and make reservations at a hotel for me. When I think about this decision—traveling on my own, to a totally unknown environment—I don't recall having any negative thoughts. I never felt afraid of the unknown. Things like health insurance considerations didn't even cross my mind, not even with my background and my health history.

We all tend to feel powerful when we're young, like nothing can go wrong. I also think I was a mature, albeit naïve, twenty-five-year-old who had opened her heart to possibilities.

After a few days at the hotel, I found a place run by the Salvation Army called the Evangeline Residence for Women at 1005 West 6th

Street in Los Angeles, dedicated since 1924 to providing young businesswomen and students a safe and affordable place to live. A room cost me about $50 a week, including breakfast and dinner. There were better (and more expensive) rooms in the renovated part of the building, but I knew I had to keep my costs low.

This place was only for women; men were not allowed past the lobby. During the time I was there, I don't remember that rule ever being broken, even though there were several failed attempts.

From then on, my life took a direction of discovery. I went to open an account at the main branch of Union Bank, a high-rise building very close to where I was staying, but I was told that I would first need a Social Security number. So I went and got one—no problem in those days. A bit later I ordered a credit card just in case I ever needed one; I got a Visa. I had no difficulty with any of those transactions.

I have always managed my money very well, and I didn't want to spend it on anything unnecessary so that I could stretch what I had brought. I decided I should start looking for a part-time job so I would have some income while looking for work in a laboratory. I started at McDonald's and also got a few hours at a pharmacy next door, on Wilshire Boulevard.

The purpose in life for most people is to have a career, a family, and, of course, happiness. When you are an immigrant, all you think about is survival. Everything else is secondary. I knew I could go back home and find a good job and enjoy a relatively easy life, but I felt the need to make it on my own, to do things my way.

Now that I think about this, I realize that my quest for survival, so to speak, caused me to digress from my initial purpose, from the dreams I had a few years prior. But I never lost my way, and I never got into trouble.

On the other hand, I think of so many immigrants who come to this country and make a big difference, how many heads of companies and others made it "big."

While I had high hopes and dreams before I had to change plans, I can't complain, as I arrived at different paths that have also given me great satisfaction.

"ON TRAVEL" (ACRYLIC ON CANVAS)

THE LICENSE

I did get homesick several times, and I decided that the best antidote for insanity would be a boyfriend. It wasn't too much later that I met a nice guy who kept me company so I could play some tennis and party a little.

I usually like to explore my surroundings when I'm in new place, whether it's living in a new city or changing work to a new area. This time, every single place was new to me. On many weekends I would take a bus from 6th Street, which was located just over the freeway from the Bonaventure hotel, very close to the Evangeline residence where I lived, to visit the very famous Beverly Hills and all the beautiful surrounding areas. I enjoyed the atmosphere around Westwood, where UCLA is located.

I would map a different route every time. I always started on the bus that went down Wilshire Boulevard, which is the most direct route from downtown to Beverly Hills, UCLA, etc. It was very easy for me to spot the places I wanted to explore and just get off the bus. I explored everything from the fancy, expensive stores in the downtown Westwood area to art galleries and museums, like the one at the La Brea Tar Pits and the gorgeous Los Angeles County Museum of Art, which are both on Wilshire. All of this was on my budget from McDonald's, since most of it was free. All I needed was a bus ticket for the day, a sandwich, and a good disposition to walk . . . a lot. I enjoyed those outings even if it meant waiting forever on a hot corner until the bus arrived at the end of the day.

On one of my bus rides I happened to pass by Cedars-Sinai, one of the best and most prestigious hospitals in Los Angeles. I decided right then that it would be nice to work there. I wasn't intimidated, because I was unaware of its famous reputation. I didn't see any obstacles.

Later on, I arranged an interview. The fact that my English was still pretty choppy didn't make me self-conscious at all. Everything went well, and I got a job in the department of parasitology. I could not believe it! I was then sent to human resources so I could complete my paperwork.

I found out that a passport and a diploma weren't enough. I needed a license as a medical technologist, which was news to me. I realized that I had not done the proper homework before I left.

Working at this hospital would never be on my résumé after all.

If I couldn't find a job at a hospital, I wanted try something else because I needed a change from McDonald's. It was driving me crazy to work there.

On one of my next trips I passed by the Beverly Hills Hotel. I thought I could easily be one of those ladies who fixed beds and cleaned rooms. But that turned out not being a good interview because I didn't have any experience.

I was getting very discouraged, so on the very same day I got off at a medical building and decided that I would go to as many of the medical offices as I could to look for interviews. At least it would be related to my background, and I thought for sure someone would be in need of help. Which turned out to be true! . . . Only to be told that I was overqualified.

I couldn't take any more rejections that day. I just sat on the stairs to let all my frustrations out and tried to regroup mentally before I got on a bus to go home empty-handed, so to speak.

Over the following weeks, I researched all the information on how to train for the licensing exam and also found a job at a laboratory in a doctor's office, where I could work with a temporary license. The owners encouraged me to go ahead with the test and bought me some books to prepare.

The first time I didn't pass. I took it a second time, still without any luck. At this point, the doctor's office was no longer allowed to keep me with a temporary license. I needed to find another job.

This time I went to one of those big laboratories that resembles an assembly line. I was able to work under the supervisor's license with some restrictions and very little pay.

But I still needed to take the test again. The basic knowledge was the same as what I had learned in school; all of my records were sent from the university in Colombia directly to the California Department of Public Health, and I was fortunate that I didn't need to take additional classes. As we all know, the field of medicine is in constant evolution, and as far as the laboratory is concerned, new tests and methodologies are implemented constantly. It was hard to stay up to date and also remember everything since I had graduated several years prior. Doing it all in a different language didn't help either.

I bought more books and studied about eight hours a day, sometimes twelve. I was totally focused without any distractions. I was able to do so because after about a year or so of working at the laboratory, I was laid off—but not before they had me train the company driver on the machine responsible for blood counts! Crazy, but true.

The equipment was simple to operate, but the person still needs to have laboratory training to operate it.

This happened a couple of months or so before the exam. Even though at the moment it felt as if the ground under me was dissolving, it was a blessing in disguise. It turned to be the best thing that could have happened, by giving me the time that I needed to study. I decided to use some savings to get by instead of looking for another job right away. (Thanks, Mom, for teaching me to make sure I had some savings available at all times!)

I ended up taking the exam four times in total, but I did it! I got my license. It was one of the happiest moments in my life. I finally would be able to enjoy stability in this amazing country that had welcomed me so warmly.

I have always been persistent.

IN BETWEEN

From the time I got my license until now, the quilt of my life has had patches of bright colors, as well as dark ones.

I found the man of my dreams, got married, worked at several good jobs, traveled, took many art classes, and had my daughter after seven years of marriage, while still in California.

I never saw myself as a stay-at-home mom, but that is how it turned out. In 1992, my husband, who was working for the auto industry, was transferred back to his home state of Michigan, where his parents and brother still lived. We were all very happy that our daughter, Monica, would grow up surrounded by family. I was very grateful that life granted us the good fortune of celebrating Christmases, birthdays, and Halloweens all together. Monica was able to collect the special memories that only family can provide. In California we'd been by ourselves. The downside of this move was that I soon found out the road ahead would not be the easiest for me or my career. I could never have imagined that my laboratory career would come to a sudden halt, as would my marriage eventually.

When we arrived in Michigan, I found out that my license wasn't valid there. One of the rules for the test that is recognized nation-wide is that a foreigner had to be living in the States for at least three years prior to taking the exam, which wasn't the case for me. So I had taken only the California test, but everyone told me that it

"CELLO (LISTEN #12)" (WATERCOLOR/INDIA INK)

"PIPER (LISTEN #17)" (WATERCOLOR/INDIA INK)

would be accepted everywhere because it was one of the toughest.

This was a hard reality to swallow. All that hard work and effort for just a few years' payoff.

I would not take the exam for the license again, because by this point I had graduated almost twenty years prior and had a six-month-old baby.

I then set out to embrace motherhood with gusto, even though I had never been the motherly type. I found great pleasure in passing on my culture to my daughter. I taught her how to read in Spanish at a very young age, and I also tried my best to transfer to her my love of art. Her father, Paul, did his best to transfer his love of music, which was so important on his side of the family.

When Monica started school, I began to pursue my degree in art at Wayne State University in Detroit. I found a job working in andrology, in a laboratory dedicated to procedures to help with infertility. There was no license needed for some reason.

Around the end of Monica's school years, her father and I got divorced.

It was a difficult situation for everyone involved no matter what. For me, it felt as if all the demons got together to squeeze all the juice of life from my body. I hurt deeply for a long time.

At the time, I was preparing for a solo show while still working part-time at the laboratory, which turned out to be a lifesaver. I went on high gear for several months, and during those difficult days I at least had a bit of a distraction. I have always felt that the watercolors I did during those days (the *Listen* series) had tears and water mixed together.

After a while, I decided to leave aside all negative thoughts and make my soul as light as a feather. This idea came from stories about

Egyptian history that I had read to Monica when she was little. After death, the Egyptian priests would take the heart out of the deceased body and weight it to see if it was heavy; only the ones light as feathers could go on to reach their final destination. I'm not sure if this is a myth.

I eventually fell in love again and married Harlan.

FOOT DROP 101

SEPTEMBER 2016

Slowly I have arrived at the conclusion that my dream of finally being free of medical issues is no longer possible. I will never be free. I have wished for the longest time to go on with my life without health worries.

I am not asking, *Why me?* My question instead is: *Haven't I paid my dues?* I feel as if I have been picked on once too many times.

Given the circumstances, the fact that I have no other worries is a big plus. I have a very supportive husband, family, and dear friends.

After almost a year since my last hip surgery, I noticed that the muscles on my right leg were not responding. I was very compliant with all the physical therapy exercises, but I still couldn't go upstairs without supporting myself on the rail with my arm. My right foot wasn't landing correctly as I walked, so I tried a shoe lift insert, but it only made me uncomfortable.

I finally decided to see a specialist. He didn't think that my condition needed much attention. "Take Tylenol . . . physical therapy . . . get a TENS machine. . . ." (A TENS machine gives the muscle a light electrical current that temporarily relieves the pressure of pain.) So I did all of that.

One day on a trip to Target, as I approached the store, I saw my reflection in the glass doors. I was walking somewhat out of balance. I paid attention, and it dawned on me that for some reason, my foot was not touching the ground the usual way.

I went to see my physical therapist of many years, and she told me I had something called "foot drop."

Foot drop is caused by weakness or paralysis of the muscles involved in lifting the front part of the foot. Causes of foot drop might include nerve injury. I needed to see the doctor immediately, which I did.

I went to see the same doctor I had seen before. This time he got visibly nervous over the signs of foot drop. He performed an EMG test that involved inserting needles on the muscles and measuring the electrical response after being given a charge of current. He told me that I would need surgery and sent me on my way to the surgeon.

I just could NOT believe this!

I don't go through those five stages anymore when presented with bad news. There is no more denial. I go straight to intense sadness. As I have expressed many times, this is nothing compared with some other people's health problems. I just need constant repairs, I tell myself. Still, all I want to do is cry. I cry while driving, while going to sleep, in the shower. . . . I guess it's a good thing not to keep anything inside. I have never been able to do that, which likely has allowed me to be calm half the time.

"ANTICIPATION" (ACRYLIC ON CANVAS)

PAINTING

It seems to me that I have enjoyed painting since I was in second grade. But my mother had forecasted starvation if I became an artist—very different from the way the current generation of parents process similar decisions.

One of the memories I have from my childhood involves my dad coming up with a device that allowed me to do my homework or paint from my bed, very similar to what Frida Kahlo's father gave her when she was bedridden. My father's invention, I remember, was a board with an arch in it so that it could sit over my chest. This piece was tied at the top to another board for support and, together, would open in an *A* shape.

Fast forward "several" years—or what seems like another life—and I have been enjoying what came to be an almost full-time occupation after my career as laboratory medical technologist.

I ended up taking a few art classes at the Otis Art Institute of Parsons School of Design (now Otis College of Art and Design) in Los Angeles. Later, I was able to enroll at California State University, Fullerton, followed by Wayne State University in Detroit after we moved. I also took other interesting classes in art centers. All of that squeezed in while I was working at the laboratory full-time.

I still needed two or three credits in order to earn my art degree, probably jewelry or sculpture or something else I wasn't interested

"INSIDE A FAIRY TALE" (MONOTYPE/COLLAGE)

in, but I was ready to get busy in search of my own style. I made the decision not to graduate.

Given that over the last twenty years, on average, I have needed a major surgery about every three years, I have had to interrupt what I was doing and leave my studio for two to three months at a time. I remember the enjoyment that I felt every time I was coming back, always convinced that it was the last surgery for good. I remember several times coming back to my studio to find my brushes colonized by spider webs, and that's how my brain felt. It takes time to spark creativity and reconnect with the muse.

Many years ago I thought that painting would be the delight of my older years. What I didn't know is how uncertain these plans were.

10 DECISIONS, DECISIONS . . .

At the end of April 2016, the spine specialist decided that I would indeed benefit from a decompression on the last two vertebrae. I had to decide when to have the surgery.

But it was going to be a great year! Following my last hip replacement in June 2015, I would finally be free of surgeries. This was the year when I would start focusing full-time on my art. No more spending half days three times a week going to physical therapy visits.

I had booked a vacation to Cartagena, Colombia, a small paradise were I would introduce Colombia to Harlan. My daughter and her roommate were all set to join us.

Monica's master's graduation was also set for the second week of May in Chicago. We had already decided that I would be going by myself because Harlan had a conflict.

I had also been accepted for a solo show in July at the Paint Creek Center for the Arts in Rochester, Michigan, where many artists who I have admired over the years have exhibited and who are a part of the center's history. Any artist would be proud to have a show at PCCA on their résumé. In addition to that, I had another exhibition with my painting group scheduled for September.

Harlan had scheduled a trip for August as well. He had started a tradition of going on camping trips with his son and five-year-old grandson. This one was to South Dakota to visit Mount Rushmore. He was very much looking forward to this next adventure, and I didn't want him to have to cancel because of me.

I thought about this for a while. I wanted to find out how urgent my condition was. I didn't know if all of a sudden I wouldn't be able to walk or my foot would go completely limp. No one seemed to think that would be the case, neither the doctor nor the physical therapist. Nerve-racking. In regular circumstances, I would have had the surgery as soon as possible. But instead I chose August 31, 2016.

I felt *very* guilty. Was I putting my health in jeopardy for vacation plans and the art show? Then another voice in my mind would whisper: *These are not ordinary plans, this is the culmination of many months of work.*

For once, I would go ahead with my life, albeit for a short period of time. But this back-and-forth would constantly go through my mind during the day and would be my last thought at night before going to sleep. I kept hoping that I wouldn't regret the decision later.

During June and July, I was able to do everything as planned. We enjoyed our trip to Cartagena to the fullest. I made it to the beach and walked (slowly) around town and enjoyed great restaurants.

The show at the Center for the Arts also went well. I got a nice letter saying that the show was among the most visited of its kind. The exhibition from our critique group was also very much a success. Many people came to the opening.

I didn't feel any advancement of symptoms during those summer months in 2016, but I was very much ready for August 31, the date of my surgery, to arrive.

A few days after my art show, I had a conversation with my high school friend Marta, who still lives in Colombia and who I had kept in contact with for all these years. One of her three children, Jaime Andres, is now a very well-regarded Harvard graduate, an assistant professor of orthopedic and spinal surgery at Albert Einstein College of Medicine. He is a spine specialist. When I mentioned that I would need back surgery soon, she immediately suggested that I talk to her son and get his opinion.

An excellent idea, I thought, so I contacted him a few days later. We had a good conversation and then exchanged some emails. Unfortunately, I could not see him personally.

After reviewing all of my reports, including the MRI, he disagreed with the need for the surgery and went on to explain the reasons. He wanted me to see someone with his similar experience and background and gave me the name of a doctor at the University of Michigan in Ann Arbor. I was added to their waiting list.

Meanwhile, just to make sure, I made an appointment to see my orthopedist, because hip surgeries, after all, are on the list of possible causes for foot drop. The visit was scheduled for August 2. On that same day, I got a call from the University of Michigan saying they had a cancellation, so I was able to see both doctors on the same day.

The doctor's conclusion at U of M was that the surgery was *not* needed. He didn't think that there was compression of the nerve in any way. This was the same opinion as Dr. Gomez's, my friend's son.

Then at the orthopedist visit, the doctor concluded that the foot drop was not caused by the hip replacements. He suggested I see the spine surgeon from his group as well as a neurologist he knew and trusted. He also ordered a brace called an AFO, or ankle foot orthosis, which is worn on the lower leg to support the ankle and foot.

The flat part goes inside the shoe, then it wraps around the leg and ties down with Velcro below the knee. It keeps the ankle in a neutral position during walking and other daily activities.

While it assists in walking, it does not support a normal gait. It is also bulky, so I can't use my regular shoes. This change was hard for me, as I had spent a lifetime getting the most comfortable shoes, boots, and sandals. All that was now unusable for me.

A few days later I saw the spine surgeon from the orthopedist group. He agreed with the other opinions: Surgery was not called for.

Now there were three doctors sharing the same opinion! No surgery needed. Harlan and I were very happy to hear this news. That evening we went out to dinner and toasted to "NO surgery!"

I called the office the next day to cancel it. I felt relieved, as if a big weight had been lifted off my shoulders.

"PINK SUNSET" (ACRYLIC ON WOOD BOARD/PRIVATE COLLECTION)

CHLOE

We found out in the first week of January 2017 that our cat of seventeen years, Chloe, had cancer. Chloe is a Ragdoll cat with blue eyes, a most beautiful coat, and a "poker" expressionless face.

The news affected me like I never thought it would. I remember hearing about other people confronting the death of a pet, but I never thought too much about it.

Chloe was the *gatito* (kitten) we bought my daughter, Monica, when she was about nine years old, to keep her company through the month of December while I went to Colombia to see my mother, who was sick with cancer.

Monica was about the only one among her friends still enjoying her dear pet from childhood.

On one occasion, as Monica was getting onto the school bus in front of our house, she saw that Chloe, an indoor cat, had managed to get out of the house. As the bus took off, Monica begged the driver to stop, but of course he could not comply with her wishes. She cried all the way to school. She was so distraught that the principal had her use the school phone to call home and ask about the whereabouts of her cat. I was able to put her at ease and told her that Chloe was safe at home.

It was hard to write a letter to my daughter about Chloe's situation. Fortunately, I had kept her up to date on her symptoms, so in a way she was prepared. The veterinarian told us that she might have days, possibly weeks, left, so hopefully she lasts until Monica arrives this Friday. (Today is Monday.) Chloe is slowly going downhill, eating less every day and sleeping longer than usual.

I talked to the vet because I had been feeling guilty about making the decision to put her down. She assured me that it was the right thing to do, adding that usually people delay it too much.

Why is it that we can't see an animal suffer, but humans are left to suffer in misery for days or months or years? It's something to think about. This involves many ethical considerations, but nevertheless it seems cruel.

12 ON A DIME

A visit to see *another* neurologist recommended by the orthopedist was scheduled for later in August. I wanted *his* opinion because it was clear that something was not right. As it happened, he would be the fourth doctor who agreed that the surgery was not necessary.

I remember when the doctor came into the room, he had a soft drink in his hand, which I thought was kind of unusual. He had a very casual demeanor and a very dirty coat, I noticed. The waiting room was spartan, hardly a painting on the wall, with very dark and masculine furniture that looked dated and old.

After reviewing my reports and examining me, he arrived at the same conclusion, that I should *not* have this surgery. He only wanted to redo the EMG. He said it didn't make sense and something could be wrong with the prior report (which had been done by somebody else).

He repeated and repeated it again. . . . He looked incredulous, and after a long time of fussing with numbers, clicks, and electrical currents applied everywhere in my legs, he stands up and says, "You DO need this surgery, and fast!"

He went on to explain his reasons: The nerve on the right leg was almost all done "dying," and the left was worse (I had no symptoms).

All of this was obviously very confusing. What could I possibly do?

I asked if December would be an okay date. No! he responds, it needs to be done as soon as possible. He felt the need to prove it to me, showing me the readings, which were like Chinese to me. He insisted that it had to be a compression on the vertebrae, something that the others and he himself a few minutes ago didn't believe was the case.

I asked about the possibility of ALS, and he was convinced it was not that, as I had a very strong upper body, and that would not be typical with that kind of disease. He was completely sure!

Every doctor had shown me that the nerve was wholesome, meaning not compressed by the vertebrae; looking at the X-rays, anyone could see there was no disruption of any kind.

Where could we go from here? How many more doctors was I going to keep asking about this?

It was very confusing. Just a few days before, I was definitely not having the surgery, and now it was imminent.

I did have intense pain in my lower back—for several years. Something had to be terribly wrong, and I thought the surgery could be the answer. Besides, the idea of getting foot drop in both legs was totally unacceptable and frightening, and in a way this doctor was offering me a way out, albeit an uncertain one. If I decided against it, and the situation deteriorated as he said it would, then I could never forgive myself for not trying.

I had canceled the date for the initial surgery, August 31, and now I needed to call the surgeon's office to tell them that I had changed my mind . . . again. It felt uncomfortable and embarrassing doing this.

As expected, the prior date was taken. They usually have a waiting period of a couple of months, but they were very accommodating and the procedure was back on schedule for September 14.

Still, I was not feeling good about the whole thing—about having the surgery and not knowing if that was the right decision. There were no guarantees, I knew that.

 BOOT CAMP

I decided that Dr. Gomez should have this painting titled *Bootcamp*, not only as a token of my gratitude for investing so much time in trying to help me out but also as a reminder to him of what patients go through. It came to represent for me a testimony of endurance, the victory over obstacles. I told him that the colors are bright because optimism needs to persist after all.

The way I see it, medicine is a form of art. I believe that's the reason why different doctors see the facts from their own point of view, and you end up with conflicting opinions.

Now, at this moment, I have to allow my body and all the changes that I have noticed lately to serve as a guide to do what is best. There is nothing else I can rely on.

"BOOT CAMP" (ACRYLIC ON PAPER/PRIVATE COLLECTION)

 MORNING AFTER

OCTOBER 2016

The days before the surgery were filled with anticipation and, well, . . . resignation.

I knew the drill: arrive at the prep room, belongings go in a bag, get the IV that makes your body temperature drop, then wait for who knows how long. Thirsty, upset, and hungry, trying hard to think about other things besides the days ahead. This time they didn't allow me to take my iPhone for some reason. Music is relaxing.

Coming out of the anesthesia takes me by surprise every time! It feels like I just went to sleep, and nothing hurts after all the medication they give you. This time I woke up in the recovery room to the discussion between the nurses about how difficult to intubate this patient was. "It has already been written in her chart," they said.

About four hours later the person from physical therapy came to help me walk a few steps. I had been alerted by everybody about the difficulty of getting up for the first time after spinal surgery, but I am a veteran. I knew exactly what to do and how it would feel. I was so sleepy, I could not keep my eyes open to listen to any instructions, much less walk. I did stand up, but then I had to go right back to bed. The therapist was very disappointed. I didn't care.

This time I was in a recently built unit at the hospital with individual rooms. There was a pleasant view of a pond, with beautiful trees in the background, and for a few short minutes it made me forget why I was there. It cheered me up.

I stayed for three very peaceful nights. I wasn't kept awake until late due to the conversations of a roommate and her family. I didn't miss the usual craziness that has been my luck several times before, like screaming patients—for real or imaginary reasons.

I also had a nice surprise from my friend Esperanza. She owns a flower shop and came in on the evening of the second day with a beautiful arrangement of fruits and flowers.

I want to remember what was nice in the middle of all of this, so my friend's visit and the nice room were the highlights of the experience this time.

15 SOME POLITICS

Today I was able to be with Chloe. Harlan put the cat on top of the washer so that I could brush, hug, and cuddle with her without having to bend over. We were missing each other.

I did not plan ahead any entertainment as I have done before all my past surgeries. I used to collect books and other materials, like interesting articles that I have meant to read but have not had the time to. I also made sure I had available a good and long TV series. During the downtime after other surgeries, I have watched *I, Claudius*; *The West Wing*; and *Rome*, a British-American-Italian historical drama series for television. (I really enjoy history . . . lots of drama!)

I was at a low point and didn't feel like getting anything ready. I felt exhausted after so many weeks of changes, decision-making, and doctor's visits.

Brushing Chloe took me away from watching too much politics and the constant wars in the media between Hillary Clinton and Donald Trump, who wants to make America great.

Many people who live in this country have no idea of how great things already are here and how much better our lives are compared with those who live in so many other countries. "Great" is being able to have freedom of speech, to be able to live to our fullest potential, to work hard and "make it," achieving anything you dream about if you really set your mind to it.

"WE ARE ALL RELATED" (ACRYLIC ON CANVAS/
STRATHMORE HOTEL COLLECTION, DETROIT)

I finished a book the other day, *Far and Away*, by Andrew Solomon, a journalist and experienced traveler. I learned intriguing, interesting, and even hilarious facts about other countries—some of which I had to look up on a map, I hate to confess. I also learned about nations where the majority of the population suffers from depression, as in Cambodia. Abusive governments and segregation still persist in many countries.

We have our share of problems here, but I still believe we are privileged in so many ways.

16 MAMI, YOU LOOK SO HAPPY!

SIX WEEKS AFTER BACK SURGERY

I sent some photos to my daughter the other day and received back this message from her: "Mami, you look so happy."

After reading that, I thought it was ironic to look "happy" after spine surgery, but, yes, I was extremely pleased to have all of it behind me, both the surgery and the days afterward when I could hardly move.

I am in another place now. Finally, I am ready to do the best I can to lift myself up, physically and mentally. The truth is that under the circumstances, there is so much to be thankful for. If this was my destiny, I have the best tools to deal with the situation: a dedicated spouse and family who make sure everything is all right. I am lucky enough that I have good insurance, and I'm not missing work and income due to recuperation. My only job is to heal, and that makes me a lucky person.

Harlan had taken some photographs on my first day in my studio after my post-op visit to the doctor. Now I am allowed a bit more freedom and I can start trying to do the things that I enjoy doing. I was wearing a cheerful pink T-shirt and had my painting apron on, and that alone, that small fact, had a lot of meaning for me.

17 UNABLE TO REFUSE

The much anticipated twelfth week post-surgery finally arrived.

The good news was that my spine was doing great. Unfortunately, my legs were not. The doctor implied that the reasons for the weakness and lack of progress with my foot drop were probably neurological. Besides, my "good foot" was presenting the same symptoms as the right, which means that I will end up with foot drop in both legs at some point.

I realized after all that the four doctors against the surgery were right. There was no reason to have gone ahead with it; they all agreed that the nerve was not compromised by the spine. As a patient, it is impossible to always make the right decision, especially when there is even a small possibility that the present situation can be fixed.

If I had decided against the surgery, I would be blaming myself for the rest of my life, constantly asking myself "what if." Still, I feel that something good came out of it since the strong pain in my lower back is gone. In exchange, I can no longer tie my own shoelaces.

The doctor's advice was to keep doing physical therapy and see the neurologist.

My therapist had been wanting me to add pool therapy and asked me again if I was up to it. I had been avoiding it, and she knew it. I don't think she was aware of the reasons for my insecurities. I agreed to go through with it, while deep inside, I knew I should have rejected the idea once again.

The slippery surface around the pool made me very nervous, as would the wet dressing room floor. How would I manage? I have a hard enough time walking on wood! I ordered special shoes to use in the water, but they didn't arrive on time. I never liked going barefoot in public showers and usually wore flip-flops, but those were out of the question now, as they have become a hazard.

The night before going to the pool I went to bed upset and got up just as uncomfortable. I was upset the entire time it took me to get to the gym. I could not get my mind off it.

My toiletry bag was heavy, which made it difficult to balance my cane on the other hand. I made it to the front desk to pick up a locker key and then walked down what seemed like a mile-long corridor to the changing room.

I did NOT want to be there!

I survived the dressing room and went out to the pool walking like a cat that is pushed against its will to the water. I sat on the bench . . . and started to cry. Really hard. I felt like a little kindergartner on the first day of class.

I was extremely embarrassed. The therapist was worried that I was in pain. I composed myself a little, but I cried on and off during the whole session.

I was scheduled to go back in two days, and it went better. I had the water shoes and had learned a few things from the first experience. I didn't cry, but I still never felt comfortable during the pool sessions. I am also not feeling any improvement so far in terms of my walking; it feels worse by the day.

18 MEDITATE?

It seems like a lifetime since the surgery. A lot has happened since then. I need to meet the challenges and understand the best way to deal with them.

I had hopes that I now know were unrealistic. The issues with my legs continue to go in the wrong direction.

I have to avoid worrying about what is going to happen in a few months or years. It just ruins the "now." But that's not an easy task, because controlling the mind is extremely difficult for anyone.

I have tried meditation before; I have plenty of books and recordings. Getting distracted is perfectly normal, as I am beginning to understand. Meditation tames the mind *and* it takes practice. It's the same as working out—we need consistency.

By chance while watching an interview on TV, I found out about *10% Happier*. I was curious and decided to borrow the book on audio. It was very interesting to learn about the experiences of Dan Harris, a TV anchor who suffered a panic attack during one of his broadcasts.

I especially liked the way in which he arrived at meditation. He went on a quest that took some time of personal discovery. He got in touch with experts in the meditation field, like Joseph Goldstein and Sharon Salzberg.

The benefits of meditation have been well established. It has had a big impact on sports, it's being taught in the army and in schools, and corporations are facilitating the practice for their executives to enhance their mental well-being.

I think that life often presents you with the right tools at the right moment.

My husband and I have known each other for about six years now, during which time I've gone through three major surgeries (two hip replacements and a lumbar fusion, each with a recuperation of eight to twelve weeks). We have also sold two houses, built a new one, and moved. Each of those circumstances is a major cause of stress.

To be mindful is one of the most helpful tools as we try to control our emotions. This is the base that makes the rest happen. Latin people are not very known to be in control of their emotions, and I recognize that I react to circumstances before thinking.

Health issues are a source of stress. I feel that I am constantly on the edge.

MY COLORS ARE FADING

Good wishes come and go, time to celebrate. Needless to say, I don't feel like celebrating anything, even though I recognize that compared with other people's misfortunes I can count myself among the lucky ones. Nothing hurts. But I feel that I am fading emotionally; I don't feel like talking much.

I still don't know what is happening with my body.

My left foot is getting worse, and it will need a brace as well. I am walking with great difficulty and get tired quickly. I feel as if my legs don't have the strength to hold my body. I have Googled all of my symptoms over and over, and it doesn't look good. I am now going to the gym three times a week and to the pool two times a week first thing in the morning. I have an MRI scheduled for the brain and thoracic area in a week.

I have finishing getting my studio cleaned up and old stuff put away. I am ready now to start painting again. I feel enthusiastic but also feel afraid. The unknown and unresolved health issues are a constant weight on my shoulders that I could compare to sitting next to a big monster that is ready to get me at any moment.

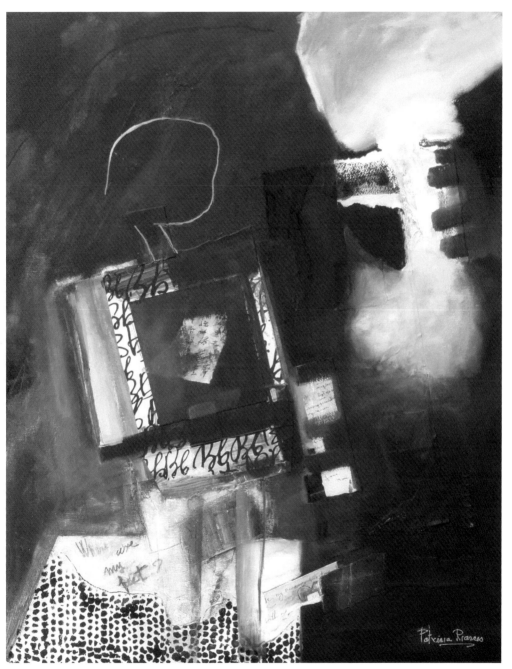

"WHAT DID YOU DO TO MY FEET" (ACRYLIC ON CANVAS)

20 NEED TO BE PREPARED

A couple of days ago, I fell for the third time. I have almost no balance and no way of catching myself if I take a wrong step. I was just a few feet from the basement stairs, so it was very fortunate that I fell down the opposite way.

Luckily, the floor is wood, and I wasn't hurt badly. Harlan was close by to help me get up.

Today I was thinking that it is just a matter of time until my next fall. Who knows where I will be—on the street, on the stairs? It's easy to kill yourself this way.

I sat down to write a note to Harlan and Monica with instructions about where to find things and stuff that needs to be done. It can happen any time. In a minute, things can change, and I can be gone just like that.

I still have to revise my will with last-minute corrections. I also have a notebook with all my passwords and places where important things can be found.

I have decided to be prepared.

21 EASY TEARS

I do try to be brave, to be optimistic and avoid obsessing. I repeat to myself that it is not the end of the world, and there are many more people with bigger problems. Still, it seems like I have tears just waiting to go on a cascade for the smallest reason.

I was at physical therapy doing my exercises. I was probably not doing them exactly right, and one of the therapists came by to tell me in what I felt was a stern voice that I wasn't trying enough. It took all I had not to burst into tears right there in front of everyone. I always try my best to do the exercises.

Even if we all think that it's just a matter of time to get used to a new normal, there are other elements that are included in the mix. It's not about what I can or cannot do, it's about how much help is needed to do the simplest of tasks.

Sometimes I give up for a while and sink into thoughts that I am supposed to avoid. I catch myself starting to list all of the things I can't do anymore, when I know I need to emphasize the ones I can still do.

It bothers me that I can't "pull my weight" around the house. Even in subtle ways, little by little, Harlan is having to do more. One of the problems is my inability to stand for a while, so washing dishes or preparing food is no longer an option.

BIRTHDAY

Today, my birthday, didn't start well. I woke up around 2:30 and could not get back to sleep. I have a busy schedule and hope that I can keep my energy up. It's getting more difficult day by day, especially since I got a brace on my other leg a month ago—a decision made because I would have kept falling otherwise. It feels very awkward, as if I am walking on stilts. I hope I can get somewhat used to it soon.

I am going to visit my friend, the physical therapist who helped me with most of my recuperations from past surgeries. Even though I am officially going to a really good therapist in the orthopedic department at the hospital, I want to talk with my friend to see what she thinks, if she has some ideas.

I had not seen her in a long time, and she was very surprised to see me walking with such difficulty. She didn't have much more to say after all, but she encouraged me to keep seeking an answer and gave me the name of a doctor whom I had actually seen many years ago.

I didn't know it then, but going to see him would eventually be the key to finding an answer.

MISSING CHLOE

Chloe was put to sleep several weeks ago (on January 10). I sent my friends and family an email with some photos.

I never thought it would be so hard. I feel like I am blowing things a bit out of proportion, but her passing comes at a time when I am in limbo and nothing makes sense. I miss her coming to the door to greet us like a dog, her waiting by the bathroom door to go lick the water after someone showers, and many of the unique traits that a make a pet part of your life. She represents at this moment a face-to-face encounter with death, emptiness, and loss.

Monica drove five-plus hours from Chicago to be able to take her personally to the vet for the final moments. We spent that evening holding her and talking to her as if she could understand why we were so sad. Monica was stronger than I was. Nowadays I am overly sensitive.

The three of us went to the vet's office. Monica carried Chloe all wrapped up in her favorite blanket, her eyes closed and very quiet as she made the transition into the doctor's arms. Neither of us wanted to be present as she received the injection.

24 FOCUS ON THE NOW

It's the beginning of April, now three months since I last saw the physical therapist treating me after the back surgery. She gave me a complete program of exercises to do at home. I went to see her again the other day, and we both were very surprised at how everything is actually worse.

I got the impression that she had run out of new things to try, but she came up with a different idea—a contraption involving some ropes that hang from an apparatus as high as the ceiling. It is supposed to force some muscles to "fire up" in a different way. Harlan, with his usual sense of humor, thought that sounded exciting and asked if we could install one in the bedroom.

He has been able to keep my spirits up by looking at the bright side of the things and making the weirdest and funniest comments so that I don't take life so seriously.

I was thinking today what a good decision it was to have gone on the trip to Cartagena last year. That was such a fantastic trip and the perfect timing. At the time I felt a little irresponsible, but now I think that it was the right decision. As Ernest Hemingway said, "The only value we have as human beings are the risks we're willing to take." I don't agree with the word *only*, but I feel good anyway. Hemingway would have been proud of me. . . . Picture me smiling. . . .

I have to focus on *now*.

If I find myself thinking thoughts that are not helpful or positive, I force myself to let go of them. I need to change channels, so to speak, to think encouraging thoughts, remember nice moments, think of the good things I have. . . .

25 EASTER

This is Easter weekend. In Colombia, when I was young, we didn't celebrate this holiday. We were raised Catholic, but we never made a big deal about Easter. We observed Lent, and that was about it. No colored eggs or bunnies or any kind of fuss—it wasn't a custom then.

I don't remember celebrating when we lived in California either, but then we moved to Michigan, when Monica was a few months old, and having a child means you celebrate close to everything, whether it's tradition or not.

We got together every year to celebrate Easter at her grandma's (my former mother-in-law's) house. This kind of holiday never passes by without my thinking about her. It's not about Easter anymore, though; now it's about grandmother's memories

She had a menu that she followed strictly. I always enjoyed her fruit salads, but I didn't like her "crossed eye" buns, as I used to call them, which she thought was funny. I went to the bakery the other day, and they were advertising special dates for people to order them. It brought back the memories of our time together as a family. I get sentimental about that, no matter that we have all moved on.

Have a great Easter, everyone, whatever you are doing. . . . I reversed back to not celebrating now that Grandma is not here anymore and Monica is a grown-up.

26 THERE MIGHT BE LIGHT AT THE END OF THE TUNNEL

A physiatrist treats a wide variety of medical conditions affecting the brain, spinal cord, nerves, bones, joints, ligaments, muscles, and tendons. This is the doctor recommended to me by my physical therapist friend. I had seen him before and knew he is a good physician.

"Incomplete paraplegic" was written on the orders that he sent for the CT scan of the chest. It felt so crude and cold reading those words. I never thought of myself as a paraplegic, but there it was in black-and-white.

I looked it up. Even though the meaning is somewhat obvious, I wanted to understand the medical term literally. It means that there is a lesion on the spinal cord that has not been completely severed, and the brain can still send signals to the lower extremities.

The doctor ordered several tests, including another MRI, and also gave me a referral to another doctor in the neurological department of the University of Michigan, someone very well regarded—the head of the department for the last thirty years, with a distinguished "pedigree." If they can't figure out what it is that I have, I will be out of luck. When I called to make the appointment, I discovered that she has been on sabbatical for six months and will not be back until July (it is the end of May now). The office is scheduling for September. How discouraging.

The physiatrist also wants me to have a muscle and nerve biopsy of the right leg, a report he thinks will be useful to the U of M doctor.

I felt like screaming at the top of my lungs. Please, no more procedures!

"WAITING" (ACRYLIC ON WOOD BOARD)

27 A SHORT OUTING

It felt refreshing to go out on a beautiful, sunny, and breezy day just for mundane errands—not doctor appointments or physical therapy. I almost felt back to normal while driving, even as it was starting to be uncomfortable.

I realized that if I went early enough, before many of the businesses opened, there were parking spots available in front of the places I needed to stop.

As I got out of the car on my first stop, I had a dilemma: There was no ramp. I looked around, and there was no one to ask for help getting up the curb. I felt very insecure using the cane, but this time I had to tackle it the best I could.

The fact that I *could* still go out shopping meant freedom and some kind of normalcy. I almost forgot that my pace, as I pushed my three-wheeler little walker, was that of a small child. Painfully slow. I didn't care.

After exchanging a pair of shoes, I stopped to buy lunch.

I was extremely tired when I arrived home. I had to lie down and put my feet up. I felt good nevertheless. Harlan by now anticipates a lot of my needs. My bed was already set with cushions in the right places for me to have a good rest.

28 A CHALLENGE

I decided to visit my sister Marcela in Milton, Ontario, who had recently moved into a new apartment on her own. I had been wanting to visit for a while, and I wished I could have helped with the move. It is about a four-hour drive from my house if all goes well. It sounds a bit scary for someone unable to stand up hands-free. I knew that eventually I would not be able to drive, so this would be the perfect time to go. Personally, I did not feel uneasy. Even though the rest of my family was concerned, I knew I could pull it off.

Traveling implied carrying additional gadgets. The walker, the cane, portable handles for the bathroom, and a small rubber mat for the shower. It reminded me of traveling with an infant.

I met Marcela's friend Piero, a wonderful person, and the two of them took me for several outings, including a visit to Niagara-on-the-Lake, a beautiful little town aside from the congestion of the touristy side of Niagara Falls.

I had a great time and felt good about my decision.

Back at home I needed to schedule the biopsy. On the pre-op visit to the surgeon, I didn't get a good feeling or a good first impression. He didn't volunteer much information, and I wanted to know as much about the procedure as possible, so I pressured him for some answers.

After my insistence, he revealed that my foot would be numb for good because the nerve would be cut, a chunk "like this" (showing his fingers), so I would no longer have feeling! This sounded very radical and made me upset; I know of other people who have had similar biopsies and did not have any big side effects. I don't exactly feel like adding one more thing to worry about.

The next day I made arrangements to put off the procedure until later; maybe after the next appointment I wouldn't need it.

I found out later that I made the right decision. My extensive experience in the department of doctors, procedures, and tests has taught me that there is no obligation to follow blindly whatever it is that the doctor wants done. First you need to understand completely what is needed and why.

Of course, thinking about my back surgery, I didn't follow my own advice. Sometimes there are mitigating circumstances or excuses that we allow ourselves. What is important is that you know exactly what you are doing and understand where it is going to take you.

 RESILIENCE

I'm still trying to meditate, and little by little I've made some prog-ress. Not only does it quiet the mind, but it also helps push aside negative thoughts. I find comfort in the useful advice of the medi-tation teachers on how to practice and how to make subtle changes in my daily living.

The meditation I did today is called "The Truth of Change," by Sharon Salzberg. I am still using the 10% Happier app.

Change is a constant in life, especially as we get older. Starting new, moving, or learning new things at work is different from learn-ing to cope as you see your body refusing to respond.

As I listened to the meditation, Sharon explained how every-thing is transient and ephemeral. Then she continued to say some-thing like, "Change also brings new beginnings, doors open, second changes, not much in life is a straight shot, and one of the most po-tent aspects of beginning is resilience, the act of beginning again." So true, as we try to carry our challenges and look for ways to make them less harsh and heavy. After a while, I started to wonder If I could actually put all of those promises to work to benefit my pres-ent situation.

At the end of the meditation, she gives the advice to remember your deepest aspirations, what you are capable of, and how you define happiness. She says to remember the skill of beginning again, and see how much kindness and presence you can bring.

I need to redefine "happiness."

I am working on a personal plan to reinvent myself, to reach the world literally from a chair. Walking feels as if my legs are attached to cement blocks or those flippers that deep-sea swimmers wear on their feet.

From December to April I have observed more changes physically. These physical changes cause me to feel like I can't keep up emotionally. I have to work hard to be able to apply all the good advice given in the meditations.

30 ON MY OWN

I remember when I was pregnant, every morning I would wake up in awe, incredulous that I was actually carrying a human being inside. These days, every morning as I get out of bed and touch the floor, I want to believe that nothing has happened and this is all a bad dream.

Harlan left on Thursday to meet his son and grandson, who is now six, for their weekend of "roughing it" up north at a campground by the lake in Michigan. At this time of the year (barely the end of May), there is also all the solitude you could wish for.

I have been doing well, even though it feels like I am weaker in my knees as time passes. But I had not fallen down for a while, so Harlan seemed very comfortable leaving, and I didn't feel too apprehensive either.

On the first day he was gone, I got up to go to the bathroom without my braces. I can usually grab on to doorknobs and touch the wall for balance, but my left foot just twisted outward by the ankle, and down I went like a big sack of potatoes. I have always fallen either on carpet or the wood floor. This time it was tile. I remember thinking about it in that split second as I was going down.

I crawled across the bathroom toward the bedroom but had to wait for a few minutes until my foot could stand the pressure of my body again. My right thigh and right arm seemed to have carried the brunt of the fall (the side that had sustained three of my four hip replacements). I was very shaken. I was supposed to go to lunch at noon with my friend, but I was sore and upset and it was getting late. I called to cancel and did not mention the fall. When I talked to Harlan later on, I didn't mention it to him either. There was nothing he could do, and besides, I didn't want to worry him since he was supposed to leave for Alaska in a couple of weeks for his daughter's wedding.

Everything else went well, and I realize now that I have to use the walker permanently inside the house. I have to be extra careful. All I need is to break a bone for things to go downhill in all sorts of ways.

PROUD

Several months ago I approached the owner of a gift store about my artwork, and she agreed that I could bring it in on consignment.

I packed several boxes with small paintings and put them in the car. I didn't know if there would be parking at the front of the store, or at least close to it. Would the sidewalk have a ramp? How was I going to carry it all when I could barely hold myself with my cane?

I am of the opinion that sometimes you have to go through things and see what happens or how things evolve. Most of the time, you can trust strangers to be helpful. I was hoping that the lady at the store would help me get everything from the car if she wasn't busy, and I was also counting on finding a parking spot right in front of the store so she wouldn't have to leave it unattended while she helped me. A lot of things needed to be just right . . . and they were.

My plans were kind of risky, but there was no alternative. I can no longer pack the car and go like I used to. Now I need to count on being lucky that everything is just right, and I also need lots of planning . . . otherwise I have to start asking for help with everything I do. The thought of that mortifies me.

"JOY" (MIXED MEDIA ON PAPER/PRIVATE COLLECTION)

32 DIFFERENT APPOINTMENT

Yesterday I had an appointment for a mammogram. Since I have had two prior biopsies, I belong to the high-risk "special group," and the doctor wanted a 3-D mammogram.

The appointments are given three months in advance because there they are in high demand, and the special equipment needed wasn't yet in all the offices. I imagine they cost the same as a very nice house. I was supposed to be there at 9:20, so I got up very early since everything I do takes three times as long now. The hospital is about half an hour from home, and I couldn't park very close. The office was at the opposite end of the parking structure, so it took me a while to get to the registration desk. While I walked, I saw my reflection in the windows as I went through the corridor, and I tried to improve my gait, without much success. I tried to walk faster, but my legs wouldn't cooperate. I am noticing lately that my right leg doesn't lift more than two inches.

I finally arrived at registration and took a seat after handing in the order at the desk. The lady called me after a few minutes to tell me that my appointment was for 9:20 . . . at night! I don't remember discussing this when I made the appointment.

I did get a bit upset, but after a few minutes I just took it as another of those things that happen, just the way it goes . . . and that long walk? Well, I need exercise, and there's nothing else I could do. I am learning and trying to be at peace with the things I can't change. . . .

I went back at night, and after arriving a bit earlier I found better parking and got out of my appointment very fast. On my way out, I saw that they have valet parking right in front of the registration office, but I still think that the exercise did me good.

The results will be ready in a couple of days. I am hoping that my legs are still the "only" part of my body to worry about.

33 FINALLY AN ANSWER

In July 2017, the day of my appointment with the head neurologist at the University of Michigan finally arrived. I had been on the waiting list and got lucky to be able to see the doctor before September.

I do have ALS.

This diagnosis caught me totally by surprise.

ALS, a type of motor neuron disease (MND), is a neurodegenerative disease that causes rapidly progressive muscle weakness. Specifically, the disease affects nerve cells (motor neurons) that control the muscles that enable you to move, speak, breathe, and swallow.

The causes for this disease are unknown, as are the reasons why some people get it and others don't. It affects two to five people out of every 100,000, so it is very rare. As a consequence, the research so far has been scarce, although this is changing as awareness increases. There is no cure.

Survival is two to five years from the onset of the symptoms. Some patients will last a lot longer, especially if the first symptoms start on the legs.

I had read and researched everything related to my symptoms. I had realized that this could be a possibility, even though all the doctors I saw assured me that ALS was out of the question. They couldn't figure it out since I didn't present the usual, more common signs. In other words, the neurologist who insisted on the surgery had no clue!

Nothing prepares you for such news.

We had arrived early in the morning. The hospital is located almost two hours from our home, so we had slept at a hotel the night before so we wouldn't be late due to traffic, since there was a lot of construction on the road.

The doctor spent a good amount of time examining me and taking my history. After a while, she left the room, mentioning something about starting treatment, which Harlan and I thought was odd. Later, she arrived with a nurse and proceeded to tell me: "What you have is something called amyotrophic lateral sclerosis." She looked perfectly cool saying something that she probably had said hundreds of times, news so devastating for anyone to hear.

I could tell she was waiting for me to ask her to explain the medical terminology. I responded, "Well, that's a death sentence."

She acted surprised that I knew what she was talking about, and she went on to explain that there are eight subclassifications and I have what is called "limb onset," meaning that the disease starts on the legs and arms before moving at a slow pace to other parts of the body. She said that patients might last for twenty or thirty years. As she said that, I was picturing myself living to be ninety years old and folded like a pretzel.

All I wanted to do was cry, but I held up (for a while), then I turned to Harlan and he was crying.

The nurse that had entered the room with the doctor was there to tell me how I would be included in a group of people that come to the hospital every three months on a Wednesday and see all the specialists in the field: a nutritionist, physical therapist, social worker, respiratory therapist, speech therapist, and the doctor. They will all rotate to my room over four or five hours. She would be my contact and counselor for everything ALS related.

We spent about three hours at the hospital that morning and then went to get some lunch.

I drove that day, and the trip home was difficult between crying and trying to make some sense of all of this.

"DESPAIR" (MIXED MEDIA ON PAPER)

34 NEXT

The next step was to tell the rest of my family, and the most difficult
. . . how would I tell Monica?

I wrote to my brother and sisters, as well as to my ex-husband,
who has been the best ex-husband anyone can imagine. I wanted to
tell the news personally to Monica, so we planned a trip to Chicago.

I was hoping for strength. I did not want to break down, and I
wanted to be able to explain clearly while avoiding too much detail.
I would leave it to her if she wanted to do some research later.

When I felt that it was the proper time, I was able to handle it
well—no drama, just the facts. My Pepa (as we nicknamed her) was
strong. She received the news so well that I later thought she didn't
really understand how dire the situation was going to be. Fortunately, this particular bad news came with a soft side that nothing
was going to happen immediately, that my condition would advance
slowly, giving us all time to process.

She later told us that it bothered her that she was the last one to
find out. I wanted to be close to her when she heard the news, and it
took me a few days to get the trip going.

That was one of the most difficult things I ever had to do. It
brought back memories of the moments when I received bad news
about my mother. I wasn't as strong as Monica.

35 FIRST VISIT

When I got the diagnosis a few weeks ago, the doctor said that I probably will have a very slow progression.

I did not start reading other people's stories on the internet. I had read enough before I was diagnosed. It will be better for me to slowly arrive into each new scenario on my own, versus having a pre-conceived idea of what comes next and how difficult it will be. I do check from time to time the official site of the ALS Association and am also subscribed to their newsletter. They are very helpful.

I had my first visit with all the people who will be involved in the care and monitoring of my progression. Each specialist gave me clarification on the many questions I had. Pretty much all opinions came back to the premise that every patient is different and the evolution varies from person to person.

After understanding all the possibilities and consequences of different treatments, my feelings are, at the moment, to avoid feeding tubes and any other means of prolonging life for the sake of extending it without any chances for improvement.

When I said that, they told me at the hospital that I could be depressed. They told me that it was actually unusual for a person diagnosed with ALS to feel like that. Really? . . . I found this hard to believe.

The social worker seemed worried and asked if I had any plans or have researched ways to take my own life. Well, I wish I could find the end as peaceful as possible without going through the difficult process of this condition. From that to committing suicide is a long stretch. I couldn't even do drugs because I was too chicken.

It was interesting to meet all the professionals for the first time. So far, they have no special recommendations. I had my lung capacity measured and blood drawn. Each specialist established a baseline. So far, the only part that has been affected are my feet.

This is, still, hard to believe. Surreal. I stare into emptiness often, trying to find the good side. It is my experience that most things in life arrive with a silver lining. There has to be something. . . .

 ON THIS DAY

AUGUST 2017

It's a very beautiful day in August, not too hot or too humid, with a light breeze, making it all perfect. Harlan and I went to the park close to us in downtown Rochester. It has an easy access, where I don't have to walk for long and where we can sit by the water and watch its lazy routine downward. We can hear the cicadas, although Harlan says they are "frost bugs" . . . not sure if that's the same. It brings memories from when I was about eight years old. My mother used to send me for short vacations to visit her aunt Delia, well before I was prepared to be away from home.

She lived in a small, dusty town with a very warm climate called Santander de Quilichao. The house was spacious, with a patio in the middle, where tall trees and flowering bushes were surrounded by a corridor that led to the bedrooms. No walls in between allowed us to feel the refreshing breeze coming from the nearby river during the evenings, but also left us exposed to the high temperatures of most of the day. There was a formal, enclosed living room, only open for special occasions. I remember being in that room just once.

The house was so picturesque that I remember now Tía Delia telling my mother that it was being used as the setting for some scenes in an American movie; they had to make room for equipment and movie stars causing a big hoopla in that little town barely on the map. I wish I knew the name of the movie, I even Googled, but it has been too long.

They had a cat, several hens, and the cutest small monkey that was always tied with a belt around his waist to an avocado tree located at a bigger backyard by the kitchen. The belt was long and allowed him to run "freely" through a good amount of territory. He was always kind of cranky, and I wasn't allowed to get near him, which only made me more eager to pet him.

My mother's three aunts and three uncles lived there. In the mornings, one of them would go with me to the park, where the sound of the cicadas was overwhelming. There was a church on one side of the park, a school on another, and there was a candy store in one corner with the greatest inventory I had ever seen. Every time I had the chance, I would go there to take advantage of their supply. I also made a note to myself that one day I would definitely be a proud owner of a business just like that.

During the evenings, the three brothers would gather around the radio to listen to the news, and my grandpa would let me sit by him with a small box of fabric pieces that I had cut beforehand into strips two or three inches long by one inch wide. Then I would proceed to gather a few strands of his fine white hair and tie them up with a piece of fabric. I would do ten or fifteen of those, so that at the end he would look hilarious and everybody would make fun of him. He was a fine accomplice. How I wish I had an iPhone then to take photos!

There wasn't much to do or children to play with in the area close to the house. I needed to find ways to keep myself busy.

During the day, I would find other creative activities. Sometimes I filled a bag of small confetti-like pieces of paper, and I then climbed up to the windows that overlooked the sidewalk, so that the heads of people walking by were directly under me. It wasn't a balcony—I could almost touch them. So it was easy for me to carefully deposit a small handful of the contents of my bag onto the hats of men who were wearing one.

The traffic of passing heads was only busy sometimes, but I remember how the anticipation of preparing all the elements and the planning of my project was most of the fun. I also enjoyed imagining their reactions when they took their hats off.

It seems so simple now, kind of foolish. On the other hand, I am glad that I experienced a time when kids could be creative, when we had time on our hands, instead of just sitting on a sofa, halfway hypnotized, absorbing commercials for sweet cereals or receiving ideas about all the things we need to buy.

I guess that's the origin of my obsession to delay TV watching for Monica. I also never allowed TV games, never bought them. My home was officially labeled by the teen society as a "no-fun home."

Slowly, the hot and dusty afternoons, which almost made me feel as if the days were standing still, came and went, and the date of my return finally arrived.

I see those days spent away from home, when I was still so young, as "training" on how to handle those feelings that sit by your side, as an adult, when you are longing for the cozy comfort of your parents, siblings, friends, food, and land.

The sound of those cicadas in the park by the river brought back all of those memories of my childhood at my aunt Delia's home. I had not thought about those days for the longest time!

After our outing, it was a bit late for me to start any of the projects I wanted to do. Every day my wish is to tackle one of the big items on my list before it is too late. I feel that I should be rushing to write all the letters I want to write and also take care of things I might not be able to handle later.

I know it's not practical, but still, I wish I could leave my studio well packed (I feel I "just" unpacked, as we moved less than four years ago) so that it is not a big chore for someone to clean up later. I have a lot of stuff: many art books that unfortunately I will never have the time to read; every corner, every drawer has something meant to be used later on a painting; the stamps I collected from my mother's letters from Colombia, meant to be used in a series that I have in my head; boxes and bags with special papers that I usually add as collages to paintings. I have a small fortune in art materials.

Always on my mind is the pressing question of how long it will be until I can no longer walk on my own or no longer be able to paint. There is no assurance. Every time I ask the medical team, all they say is "everyone is different."

"SUMMER" (ACRYLIC ON WOOD PANEL)

37   ATTENDING TO AWARENESS

I did some research and found a list of things used to determine if a person is depressed. I only scored three out of ten points. Sadness is a very natural reaction to these new developments. I would rather see a therapist than take medicine since that doesn't have side effects. I will be open to advice instead.

I continue semi-successfully with meditation. Whenever I take the time to sit quietly and focus on it, I enjoy it immensely. All the different aspects and the advice given by the outstanding professionals in my app are literally food for thought. I can look into the many different topics and pick something that I know is going to help, especially when it comes to finding adequate responses to situations related either to family or the stress produced by somber thoughts.

Sometimes I postpone it until I am so sleepy at night that it's of no use. I am not nearly as busy as when I could drive and go as I pleased, yet, for some reason, I feel this need to hurry, with no time to spare, which is partly true because my right hand already has three "disobedient" fingers. I drop things constantly because my thumb has very little strength. On the other hand, the lack of consistence with meditation is also an excuse. It's lack of discipline.

This happens especially if I have a painting already started or I have several projects going. Since my energy is limited nowadays,

I want to work on those as much as I can. Sometimes I am wise enough to stop for a break, and then I meditate for about twenty minutes. It is my intention to persevere.

I particularly liked today's meditation, "Attending to Awareness," by Jon Kabat-Zinn (from the app 10% Happier), about being in your space and being friends with stillness and silence.

38 PLANNING AHEAD

SEPTEMBER 2017

In many instances, the effort to plan as much as possible leaves me emotionally drained. Time is of primary importance, and when I linger too long in bed in the morning, I regret not starting my day faster because I know there will be days to come when I will wish I could get up and go as I used to.

Living with a terminal disease is like walking on a tightrope over a deep abyss, but if you think about it, everyone else is also walking the same way. The difference is fog covering that abyss—they don't see it, therefore they don't feel afraid. That idea is from the book *The Bright Hour*, by Nina Riggs. She was only thirty-nine when she died of breast cancer, leaving two young children behind.

About a year ago, Harlan and I purchased our sites in the local and most beautiful cemetery. My ex-mother-in-law and her husband were laid to rest there. This place is like no other I have seen. It has a very extensive and gorgeous set of landscaped gardens that surround the main building, two stories high with glass ceilings that let the sun touch and comfort with its warmth the shoulders of those stopping by to pay their respects or find solace in the company of those who have left us.

I have never felt intimidated there, quite the opposite: I felt very peaceful and strangely cozy, if you could say that about a cemetery.

I thought about bringing my mother's ashes here (she died in Colombia in 2000), and my siblings agreed with the idea. My sister brought my mother's ashes from Colombia; we decided that we should not leave them behind. She has rested here now since May 2016.

My mother rests on one side and Harlan will be on the other side, and I will be in the middle. Somehow a comforting thought. I like the idea of being laid to rest inside the building instead of in the gardens, no matter how beautiful they are. I have never been an outdoor girl.

I also decided to make the funeral arrangements. I don't think of it as morbid but as a chance to do things my way, and it's also one less thing for family to handle when the time comes.

Harlan and I arrived at the appointment in the middle of heavy rain, as if reflecting the mood of the occasion. What a surreal experience to go into the building where I am going to be "sitting" in the small container I just picked up a few minutes ago.

The man helping us with the paperwork gave us a tour of the place, explaining every step of the way how they organize this kind of event. There won't be a religious ceremony, just something like an open-house visitation.

We started from the entrance that will be used by visitors. Next, we were shown the main room and the place where the urn will be positioned. The book for people to sign is placed next to the little stash of "In Loving Memory," the two pages for people to take home. It's also the place where the flowers will be set and other uninteresting details.

When he was finished, we signed all the paperwork and left.

After all was done, I was thinking that it would be a good idea if Harlan made a small video . . . but then I remembered I wouldn't be able to watch it!

39 OUT AND ABOUT

OCTOBER 16, 2017

I enjoy shopping, but not necessarily buying things. The experience of being "out and about" and the lively atmosphere are my favorite. I used to buy Christmas presents year-round; when I saw something special for someone, I would get it. By the end of the year, I usually only had to get a few things more.

In October, just a few weeks before Thanksgiving, the stores are starting to get the merchandise for the holidays, so it is interesting to look around.

I knew then that soon, I wouldn't be able to do this anymore. I tried to be mindful, to be present and enjoy the experience. Being able to touch different textures, to try things on or ask questions to the salesperson is something I will miss. Sitting by a computer looking at pages and pages is not exactly "an experience" for me. It tends to make me sleepy.

I also cherish bookstores. I stopped in at Barnes & Noble, which usually brings many memories of when Monica and I used to spend many hours in the children's department, reading books and choosing the best to buy. We would get a big bag of newly released wonderful treats. There was usually a good section in Spanish that helped me reinforce the language. We ended up with a great collection that included many art books for young children that hopefully will find good use in the future.

At a very young age, Monica was able to distinguish between the different styles of famous artists. We visited the Detroit Institute of Arts often. I think Monet and Miró were her favorites.

During her teenage years, we still looked for good books and added the latest fashion and gossip magazines. We would take our just-found treasures to the Starbucks in the store to enjoy a good cup of coffee, always at the same table by the window.

"ANY GIVEN DAY" (ACRYLIC ON CANVAS/PRIVATE COLLECTION)

40 MARCELA

Marcela, my youngest sister, came for a few days to visit. It was somewhat of an exploratory trip for her, since the United States government had just granted her permanent status, or a green card, thirteen years after applying. This venture included lots of money invested and an extraordinary amount of paperwork.

Usually after waiting for many years, the applicant receives a letter informing them about the case being accepted. The person then has around six months to suddenly quit a job, sell their house, and, if they have kids, uproot them from school. Another option is to pay a substantial amount of money, on top of what is already spent, to be allowed to extend this window for two years to get affairs in order and figure out the next step in the new country. Otherwise, the time and energy invested are gone, and the entire process has to start over (as it happened for Marcela).

I feel compelled to mention that I had petitioned for my mother to come to live with me or get residency here. It took ten years . . . arriving after she had already died.

The process is not exactly straightforward.

Petitioners spend a lot of money ordering all the original paperwork that the (now former) Immigration and Naturalization Department (INS) loses over and over. It's as if this is a way to discourage applicants.

Marcela has been very helpful in every way I can imagine. She is closest to me, only about a four-hour drive to where she lives in Ontario, so it is easier for her to visit on short notice. My other sister, Vicky, lives in Nicaragua, and my brother, Diego, lives in Montana. It's harder for them to stop by, especially for a short time.

Marcela has squandered her vacation time twice to come and stay with me during surgeries. I don't have enough words to express my gratitude.

41 CIRCLE OF FRIENDS

I went to what is called the Circle of Friends at the Detroit Artists Market, a nonprofit organization with a gallery in downtown
Detroit that has been part of the art scene for many years. It's a very
meaningful place for many artists and their careers. There are many
different programs to promote and support the artist community,
and one of them is organized visits to the houses of prominent
artists or people who have had a great influence in their respective
fields as teachers or collectors. They schedule these tours four times
a year on a Friday evening.

Visiting private collections has been a very rewarding experience. It's very enjoyable to listen to anecdotes about the hosts' own
backgrounds and friendships as they relate to certain art pieces in
their collections. For the past three times, the hosts have been cou-
ples, who were both artists on different paths.

Usually the audience of about twenty to thirty people is divided,
and each group goes to a different part of the house. The home-
owners talk about the history related to their favorite work of art,
or if the piece or series is their own, they talk about it in a such an
intimate way as if to let you in on their secrets.

In one of the houses, the artist had built his own studio, quite
big, where almost every inch was occupied by different collections,
from a series of bird and bee nests that he had found on his property

to very intricate sculptures that he had made over the years. It was a place so full of art, and I wish I could have spent more time examining it in more detail.

Around the studio there was a beautiful forest and a garden that he had put together stone by stone. It was his own small paradise, and we all could feel his pride when he was talking about it.

The architecture of the artists' homes, old or new, usually plays an important part that adds to the magic of the experience.

The last time I went to one of those gatherings was with my friend Laurie, and we had a blast. She has been very kindly driving me around, especially when art is included in the plans. The place we visited had every corner of the house completely busy with artwork. The time we had allowed the hosts to go over their collection only partially.

As we left the house that night, I reflected about this being the last time I would participate in one of these great outings. It's getting too difficult; sometimes there are many stairs, and the access is not designed for walkers or wheelchairs.

Little by little, I have been forced to let go of activities that are so dear to me, that are my connections to the world. Letting go of them has been difficult.

A VISIT TO ALS OF MICHIGAN

DECEMBER 2017

I was sitting at my desk, doing what I know better not to do: anticipating situations that may never even arrive. It's not that easy to let go of those thoughts. It's consuming if you don't have the discipline to tame your mind.

Later, I had a short phone conversation with one of the representatives from ALS of Michigan. She encouraged me to visit the office because they might have equipment to lend, and I needed a better walker than the one I was using. In addition to that, she told me about a "transport chair"—lighter than a regular wheelchair, good to go out for a short distance.

The office is about forty-five minutes away. We were received warmly by a group of busy people sorting papers around a big table located in the middle of the space. The offices are located on the periphery. The corridors are plenty wide to facilitate easy access of the very large wheelchairs needed by patients with ALS.

The entire office is decorated with the pictures of what they call "PALS"—persons with ALS. I wondered if you get your photo there only after you die. I wanted to stop and look at each one of them; there were so many. There are encouraging signs everywhere that should lift visitors' spirits.

"LOOSE ENDS" (ACRYLIC ON CANVAS/HENRY FORD COLLECTION)

After picking up the equipment, the lady asked us to step into her office to sign the paperwork. After that, she went on to explain how they will be there for me at every step of the way on this very difficult journey. They offer all forms of help possible, from support groups to classes to equipment. She went into some detail describing computers that you can operate with your eyes or how a person can write sentences by just moving her head, because that is the only part that is mobile.

She also described how they can help when the patient has difficulties swallowing, and she said a few words about tracheotomy, feeding by tubes, and so on. In just a few minutes she reminded me of the sadness and difficulties that will be coming my way.

I have never been compelled to participate in support groups. People gather with very good intentions of sharing and exchanging good ideas, etc., but I think that it would make me sad to listen to the stories of others. Most people benefit from this though.

This visit should have been comforting. I met a group of people extremely dedicated to the service of patients with ALS. I was assured that I would not have to do this alone.

Yet I felt the loneliest and became very upset. Over time, I should be better able to deal with these kinds of interactions, and I will cultivate my relationships with all the strong and dedicated people—a lot of them volunteers—helping those with this condition.

I found out that there are about four hundred people with ALS in Michigan, the second highest number of cases in the country after New Jersey.

So far no one knows why or how a person contracts ALS. Some cases, only about 10 percent, are hereditary.

43 LUNCH WITH A FRIEND

I had lunch with a friend, Deb, who is also an artist and just a couple of years older than I am.

I have been touched by all the love and warmth of amazing friends. Each person reaches out in her own unique way to communicate her concern and willingness to share with me a good time while I can.

We discussed the way we feel about our lives once you pass the age of sixty. We were wondering what would make each of us happy, what we could do to live a plentiful life with the time we have. Neither of us knows how long we have left, but she fortunately enjoys good health. It made her emotional to talk about this.

I would say that life at the present resembles a party where you are having a great time, and then suddenly you are summoned at the door to be informed that you need to go. You have no intention to leave, let alone be forced out. You are content where you are. The party is just starting!

44 TWO DIFFERENT APPROACHES

As Atul Gawande writes in his book *Being Mortal*: "Only now did I begin to recognize how understanding the finitude of one's time could be a gift."

I had thought often in the past about the frame of mind of people who know how much time on this earth is left for them. We all come across stories of "others" and wonder in disbelief how on earth they are able to cope. I have watched movies about people who overcome situations that for us seem unconceivable.

I guess it's a matter of comparing two kinds of realities, one that is imminent and as real as Christmas—there is no escape—and one that arrives as a surprise, a gift box that you will eventually open. On the surface, we seem to be happier with the surprise than certainty. . . . Why is that?

When we are told that we have a terminal illness, we become so saddened. Why is it that we don't realize that we have been given knowledge that for most people is elusive? We have time to get ready, time to talk to family and friends. Some people are able to travel and visit places they always wanted to see, accompanied by their loved ones, and the simplest of pleasures become intense and enjoyable. The ones chosen for a surprise are never given the chance.

We like not knowing; we enjoy the illusion that we will be able to see our children grow up or be able to be there when our children may need us later in life.

Depending on what passions percolate inside each one of us, we like to think about the future. We take for granted that it is there waiting for us. Almost a sure thing. The majority of people live without knowing how their lives will end. They are happier for the moment. They may or may not get those goals achieved. We all prefer not knowing, it is human nature. We prefer to be able to dream rather than having to plan for the end. Which is logical.

There is another element. As we find out the details pertinent to our death, we can visualize suffering, difficulties, and pain. All that in addition to leaving dear ones behind. This is what makes the announcement of our imminent death so unbearable.

I imagine it's the reason why we aren't allowed to see the future. People would give up, they would never attempt new endeavors, and half of the world would be paralyzed . . . by sheer sadness and pessimism.

Now that I am finished with all the planning, I can concentrate on doing what makes me happy. More reading, watching interesting movies, and for sure painting. I have decided that I am going to be resting from my braces at least one day a week. On Sundays I have been staying in bed and lounging all day long, working on my computer or watching art movies. I have never done that, a small but enjoyable pleasure. Also, even though I have been a bit fanatic about eating healthy, I am allowing myself to order desserts more often, another small pleasure.

On the other hand, I always thought about my own death, wondering about the circumstances, and imagined that I would have the time to get very old. I already knew the kind of clothing I would be wearing and which colors. I dreamed about the places I would visit. All while painting as much as possible since I finally felt comfortable in my own artist skin, so to speak.

This is precious time. How can I make the best of it? One thing I would like very much is to get together with family for a few days in a nice location close to the water around Lake Michigan.

I can't leave things for later. This IS later.

Another of Atul Gawande's quotes reads: "Courage is strength in the face of knowledge of what is to be feared or hoped."

45 SOME OUT-OF-THE-BLUE RANTING

FEBRUARY 2018

Many times I have received those long videos that friends send you through social media.

They can be very inspiring. They show beautiful older ladies or famous people over dreamy landscapes and, of course, lovely music in the background.

One very famous theme is "If I could do it all over again" or "If I were young again" . . . I would spend more time laughing or I would . . . I would . . . I would.

Things usually look better in hindsight. Frequently, we look back on something after several years with a smarter version of our decision. How we could have done it this way or the other. Life has provided us with much better judgment, and now we know exactly how it should have been handled.

In my humble opinion, each person responds the best he or she can in any given situation most of the time. If you didn't spend more time playing rather than working, it might have been because you couldn't or you were often tired or you worked too hard so your family could enjoy a better life. Or you were just lazy. Yes, the time lost never comes back, we should have paid attention to advice from others. Situations were different.

We all love to give advice, some more than others . . . especially about the stuff that we wish we would have done.

Have you ever tried telling your children or siblings how things work better if you do this or that? Or if you could eat what's better for you? How is it working for you as you tell your husband how something or another would be easier if only he could do things this way . . . *my* way?

Later, some will be wishing they had listened.

46 BAD PLANNING

I had been waking up with headaches and neck aches a few times a week for a long time. I wasn't sure if I should blame the pillows or some arthritis in the neck area or if this issue was related to ALS.

In any event, I wanted to try a denser pillow than the one I have. I have many bed pillows in the house, and I have I tried them all, to no avail. I was still waking up uncomfortable. You could say that I fuss with pillows more than anyone you know.

I decided to order another pillow of the same brand of a couple I have, just a bit firmer. Instead of having it mailed, I decided to pick it up at the store. Not the smartest decision. I don't know what I was thinking, besides trying to avoid Harlan's picking on my obsession. I was also thinking that if I got the pillow at the store, I could press it and feel how dense it was before deciding whether I wanted to take it with me or exchange it.

My feet felt quite stiff, and I knew for sure that this was probably the last outing on my own. As I approached the counter at Macy's, I started thinking about the volume of my merchandise. How was I going to carry a big pillow in a package almost half my size in my little three-wheeler walker? I already had bought a sweater, and that, together with my purse, took up most of the space in the little bag that goes in the middle of the cart.

The lady handed me the package, and I clearly noticed that she was asking herself the same questions, even bending over the counter as if to size up the space on the walker and the size of the package. It was Christmas, and the store was pretty full; she could not possibly offer to help me bring it to the car. The thoughts I had about feeling the pillow were unpractical since it was all packed and there was a line behind me.

As I tried to accommodate the package, it wouldn't fit horizontally, so it had to go on top of the cart in a vertical position, like a tower, making it difficult for me to see where I was going.

Long story short, I didn't fall (my biggest worry), but I could hardly see my way. I looked from the right side . . . not too good, then the left . . . same. I walked very slowly while catching the pillow on its way down a couple of times. I must have been quite a sight!

It was my longest trip from the middle of the Macy's store to the parking lot. It also was the last thread of independence.

From then on, I would have to rely on the graceful offers from my dear friends if I wanted to go to art galleries or the museum or shopping. Harlan is already doing enough, and if possible, I want to avoid dragging him out on these kinds of outings.

The wheelchair is not too heavy. It's intended to be taken in the car, but the foot rest accessories need to be put on and off every time. Even if I am just over one hundred pounds, it adds up if we get out of the car more than twice. It is a bit of a workout for anyone by the end of the day.

"SEARCHING FOR THE RIGHT PILLOW" (ACRYLIC ON CANVAS)

47 WRAPPING PRESENTS

I had been wrapping a few presents at a time for several days, so I planned to finish up that day.

As I sat at the basement table with all the supplies around, I turned on Spotify and listened to the most beautiful Baroque Christmas songs. I also found a very nice album with "The Little Drummer Boy." All the songs were familiar to me and were performed by a chorus of young boys from Vienna or something like that. "Silent Night," another of my favorites, was also on the album.

It reminded me of the early Christmas services we used to go to as a family. Both grandparents, the three of us, and Uncle Mark, as we all ended up calling Paul's brother. I remember the usual long sermon and little Monica being very patient as she usually was (but in case she got restless, I would usually bring some paper and a couple of colored pencils).

It felt good at that moment to remember the lighting of the candles and singing "Silent Night." It was always extremely cold on those nights and usually snowing. For some reason, the memory of something as simple as picking out our coats from the crowded little room and waiting for Paul and Grandpa to bring the cars to the door is so vivid in my mind.

Abuela Doris, Monica's grandma, usually baked five to seven different varieties of beautifully decorated cookies. I have never before or after tasted anything even similar. They were each unique, thin and delicate. It was a tradition that we all looked forward to during Christmas. I regret never asking for the recipe, at least for Monica to continue the tradition. (I am not very good at baking.)

How nice to have those memories; they will be true and present in our minds, ready to give us a feeling of warmth whenever we want to go back in time and relive past celebrations together.

48 A TOPIC TO DISCUSS

I received a text message from Monica. Stephen Hawking had just died, and she was surprised to learn that he had ALS. I responded that some people don't think that he had it because he lived for so many years, and usually ALS patients have a shorter lifespan. Then I told her how those who choose to have a tracheotomy live longer because the difficulty breathing is then alleviated.

As we kept texting, the conversation developed into matters that are better discussed in person. I told her about the quality of life in that situation—the care needed when someone is on a respirator, the inability to talk—and the thousands of dollars it costs to have round-the-clock care. She was at work, and I knew if I expanded on that subject any further, she would be in the wrong frame of mind.

Nevertheless, this was a small window for me to start the conversation about my wishes for later. We have never discussed this topic: first, because it is obviously sad, and second, because I didn't want to start telling her facts that she probably didn't want to hear or wasn't ready to deal with yet.

She then told me how she was getting sad, as I had anticipated. I replied by telling her that we would discuss this further some other time, and I also mentioned that my wishes are in writing in a special document and we should talk about it if she wanted to. For now, we should focus on the present, especially given the fact that despite my symptoms having started around 2012 (as estimated), I have still been able to function pretty well. I told her how grateful I was to be able to be typing the current message to her on my iPhone.

A conversation to be continued some other time.

49 HAPPINESS

DECEMBER 2017

I was reading something that I received from my sister Vicky, who leads a very spiritual life. She seems completely at peace with herself and with those who surround her. That requires good discipline and an effort to get to know your own self.

I have come to realize that the inner peace that every person is able to reach is the important part, no matter where it comes from. If she finds extreme peace through God, perhaps that is the same peace anyone can find in other principles. God, for me, is a subject that has different approaches.

One of the readings she sent me is about the seemingly unimportant routines that we go through every day. A boring Sunday with family makes you realize that nothing is forever, as later on those simple gatherings will not be possible anymore. Or those nights that are spent with friends trying to fix the world. Life is constantly there in the smallest of things.

It is a delightful reading. It goes on to help us realize that we are rich with life. It focuses on the simple daily moments as magical pieces of a quilt.

Life is there and enjoyment is there when I can still get in the car, even if it is only to the supermarket. Or I can visit a friend's house or go out to a restaurant. I can take care of myself and handle my studio and a few other things around the house. I need to enjoy and be thankful for this small list that might seem so ordinary to everyone else. It becomes even more precious because I know it is short-lived.

Of all the things I can still do, painting is a big deal. I am grateful for this every day.

50 . . . AND ONE MORE TRIP

Women keep their friendships forever. Some men cultivate theirs from younger years, but I don't believe it is as common.

I am still in communication with a couple of neighbors that I used to play dolls with, as well as my very dear friends from high school and college. Just a handful, which makes them even more treasured. That's not to exclude from this group my dear friends I have made through the years living away from my homeland. I have never been a "party girl," but I cherish friendships, which in my opinion are one of the genuine pleasures in life.

I have not told many people about my "state of affairs" at the moment. It takes a good amount of mental energy to go through this process with each person, and it's draining and difficult not only for me but also for the friend I am sharing with. I plan to go through this slowly.

Early on after my diagnosis, I did tell three good friends from high school who still live in Colombia. One of them, my friend Marta (the mother of the spine specialist who helped me), insisted that I travel as soon as possible before it got too difficult. She owns a gorgeous chalet-style house in a beautiful location outside Bogotá, La Calera, which is located in the Andean region about 9,000 feet above sea level.

The thought of traveling had never crossed my mind. It was a crazy idea that eventually became reality, because for every hurdle I could think of, my friends had an answer. Harlan was also very much agreeable to the trip, which was important.

Marta got together with my two other dear friends, Ruth Nancy and Pilar, also from high school. The three of them organized an amazing schedule for all of us.

It felt a little crazy in my mind to attempt this adventure at this particular time, but I dived into the idea with the conviction that it would go well, that all of us would be able to take care of every circumstance, and I didn't allow any negative thoughts to enter my mind. Everyone, including the team at the hospital, thought it was a great idea. Also, I knew the window of opportunity was narrow.

I didn't announce my visit to anyone else in Colombia, given how difficult it is for me to move, plus the visit was short, and I didn't want to impose in terms of time or traveling on my friends, who were doing a lot already to coordinate my stay.

At the airport, they already had a wheelchair, which made it a lot easier for me to conserve energy and be able to enjoy every aspect of the trip. From the moment we arrived at the airport and for the following twelve days, the seven of us (including our spouses) enjoyed each other's company, with leisure and great food as the order of the day. I was able to once more lay eyes on the greenest of grass and the beautiful mountains of Colombia. I enjoyed the most delicious food, a private music performance, and the joviality that is so prevalent in the culture of my country.

I will be forever grateful for all the love and kindness that I saw in the eyes of every one of my friends and their spouses, and for how willing everyone was to help with logistics and the efforts they all made so that I could eat my favorite foods and visit places I had never even seen before. I consider myself very lucky to enjoy friendships like these.

This trip lifted our spirits. Harlan and I are immensely appreciative for the generosity and hospitality that we were able to experience.

51 ALTERNATIVE MEANS

I had plans to reach old age, painting all the way until the end. It would be the activity that would keep me busy and sustain me through all kinds of difficulties. No matter what happened, I would have the opportunity to keep creating.

It looks now like that may not be the case. My fingers, especially the thumb and the index finger of both hands, are experiencing "technical difficulties."

I am rushing to finish one last big painting, forty-eight by thirty-six inches, that I had started months ago; since my attention had to be focused on other matters, this unfinished canvas has been sitting against one wall in my studio for a while. I dislike leaving stuff unfinished, especially paintings.

I decided to tackle it the other day. It was a very challenging endeavor, because it's impossible for me to stand in front of the easel like I used to, as I have completely zero balance. I have a comfortable high chair that for some reason won't go down. It's stuck. I thought about buying a new one, but then I wonder how much longer I will be in front of the easel. Time is the main thing that I have to consider before making any decisions.

While I sit on a small office chair, I get the canvas off the easel and set it on the floor so that I can reach the top part of the canvas, then I get the painting back up on the easel again to get to the bottom of the painting. Doing this several times is a workout. But the painting is coming along, and during the process I don't think of anything else. I forget for some precious hours what is happening to me, that nothing is normal anymore, and my mind is busy and focused on creativity.

There are other challenges. I tried switching to my left hand, where my fingers are a bit stronger. So far I am managing. Maybe it will be easier once I start working smaller; it will be less physical. I promised myself to persevere for the longest time, to always find a way to keep going.

P.S., once finished, I decided to name this painting *Focusing On the Positive*. Kevin, the man who bought it, wrote this to me in the process: "Not only do I find it captivating, but the title struck a chord in me. I am constantly thinking that my wife, Sharon, whom I also find captivating, is always focusing on the positive. She is definitely an optimist! I would like to consider buying this painting to celebrate our thirty-fourth wedding anniversary."

This was so significant, it moved me to tears—that my intentions and the title of the painting delivered precisely the message that moved me to create it. This adds such relevance as I paint, knowing that the internal feelings that move me to create end up producing such a special reaction from the viewer.

"FOCUSING ON THE POSITIVE" (ACRYLIC ON CANVAS)

 ## ANOTHER BIRTHDAY

A bad thing and a not so bad:

The bad is that on my birthday last year, I was still struggling to find out what was wrong with me and was very discouraged. Now at least I understand what I am dealing with and what to expect—which is as difficult in a weird, twisted way.

In any event, I did celebrate life! On several occasions. My Colombian friends Maria Teresa and Esperanza took me out for lunch. Esperanza, the one who is a great floral artist, brought me a gorgeous flower arrangement.

This birthday marks the month when I decided to no longer drive. My wings have been cut off. We sold one of the cars, and now there is room in the garage for an eventual ramp for easy access.

Nothing needs to be added here to mark the significance of the occasion.

IN SICKNESS AND IN HEALTH

Since I have already gone through a divorce, I often make mental notes about mistakes not to repeat, things that could break the balance of a good marriage. I want to make sure that nothing bothering us is kept unmentioned.

When the contributions to daily life in a marriage are not balanced, it can be taxing for the person with most of the burden.

Lately, I get tired even as I stand to brush my teeth. Harlan has been slowly assuming all the responsibilities for grocery shopping, cooking, and washing dishes. I can still do some laundry, and so far, I don't need any personal help with bathing or getting dressed. I also water the plants and fight for my "right" to wash a couple of dishes once in a while.

From time to time I ask him how he is doing, how he is holding up, if he thinks that life has dealt him a bad hand—and I tell him how sorry I feel about this. I want to know if he can think of something else that I could do to help.

His answers are always reassuring. His response this time: "During sickness and in health, until death do us part, remember? If it was me you would be doing exactly the same."

It is not that easy to be constantly on the receiving end, and I am extremely appreciative that I can count on him always.

I know that things are not as difficult as they are going to be. I know that our daily life and routines will be getting more complicated as my condition advances.

54 TO MONICA

My Monica, this has been a difficult journey for all of us. As a daughter myself, I identify with your feelings. I remember the time when I found out about my mother. I was in my forties, and it hit me hard. There is not an easy way to be prepared for whatever there is to come. No matter how old you are, you are never ready. I hope that we still have a long and meaningful time to enjoy each other.

I try to deal the best I can. I am grabbing onto all the ingredients of daily life that keep me functioning. At the time I am writing this, I am still able to paint, to hold a book in my hand and turn the pages, and I can still dress myself and enjoy a good steak or an arepa.

I often feel extremely sad. There are times when I wonder what is the point, why keep going, what is my purpose. Then all of the sudden, you call just to say hi. Or you send me a text message asking what I think about your getting an Apple watch.

Then I decide that as long as I am alive, I can and will be there for you to share either silly or important issues. *Son esas pequeñas cosas* (it's those little things) that make life worth it and lift the spirit.

You have been the doll I played with and the little sick kitten that kept me awake at night. You absorbed my culture like a sponge. You allowed me to "inject" in your soul the love for art. I can see that now. You also tolerated with resignation my obsession to instill in you the quest for knowledge, to awaken your curiosity, like the time

I made you do a research paper about the Nobel Prize. Or how I wanted you to do the best you could, no matter how simple the task, even though you wanted your teacher in second grade to make me understand that a C grade was just fine.

Now that you are a grown-up, I sit back and admire your judgment and the way you handle the challenges of life.

"SUMMER DAY LUNCH" (ACRYLIC ON CANVAS)

55 TO HARLAN

We were married for less than five years when we found out the news. We took one vacation where we were able to enjoy everything without restrictions of any kind. The rest of the times, there was always something, and planning any kind of adventure became complicated. We nevertheless were able to squeeze in some time away because we dared to be brave and made the best of it. Thanks ever so much for your patience with those issues.

No one anticipates the future, but you certainly have been able to handle whatever life has placed on your shoulders. We have adjusted together. Your good sense of humor and optimism has certainly made this journey a little easier.

I have enjoyed the introduction to live pipe music. It has always been a pleasure to hear you practice.

"PARADE DRAWING" (INK)
My birthday is the day after Saint Patrick's Day. Harlan made for me a
drawing of himself and Chloe.

 FAMILY REUNION

I mentioned early on in these essays how I wanted to get together with my family, maybe somewhere by Lake Michigan. We were fortunate to be able to make this happen.

But first, two weeks before our getaway, I enjoyed a short visit from my sister Vicky and her husband, Amilcar. They made a special stop to visit us on their final days from other destinations on their way back to Nicaragua. I am very appreciative that at least we saw each other, since they could not join us by the lake. Marcela surprised us also, and we, too, were able to enjoy memorable hours together. I have been recording in my memory these precious times as well as I can.

I was glad that I was able to find a beautiful property with a private beach on Lake Michigan that was *also* totally handicap accessible (the owners have a son who uses a wheelchair).

This trip took place at the beginning of fall 2018. It was an immensely rewarding experience, especially through the eyes of someone who is uncertain about the immediate future in so many ways, including in terms of being able to move around, much less being able to enjoy the company of family living so far away.

The house was very cozy, but also spacious, with a big window that looks directly onto the lake at a very close distance. There were multiple amenities for a person in a wheelchair, including several ramps. One of them took me about five feet from the water, so I was able to hear the slow reach of the waves methodically announcing their presence with their rhythmic approach to the sand. The weather couldn't have been more comfortable, and the sunsets—famous at Lake Michigan—did not disappoint. I have always enjoyed the water; I would have been taking one of the kayaks for a ride in normal days. But at this moment just being there and seeing everyone enjoy their time filled me with happiness.

During our stay, I felt a warmth coming from everyone, hanging in the air almost like the little drops of dew that you can touch everywhere when you go out to a garden early in the morning. I felt very pampered; I enjoyed every minute of family time. I hope each person realizes how much it meant to me every time they came to my room when I was taking a bit too long, to see if everything was all right, or when I was offered tea and they made sure it wasn't steeping too long. I accepted most of the martinis, Bloody Marys, and wine that my brother, Diego, offered. We were all in the mood where everything anyone says or does is incredibly funny!

It was a delight to see Diego for the first time after so many years. We all enjoyed his joyous personality, especially his performance abilities by the bonfire. I want to keep each one of those memories as part of the repertoire that I will need to reach into to cheer myself up later on during this difficult journey.

Special thanks to Amilcar Daniel, for traveling from California to share time with his aunt and other relatives, also to Sarah for squeezing in time away from work. Marcela and Piero, Monica and Bennett: Thanks for your time spent with me. Every moment I spent in your company was special.

57 HUMOR

I was thinking the other day that humor is a good way to escape reality. It's free, and it does a ton of good to the body and soul.

I have been living here in the States for longer than I lived in Colombia. Anyone absorbing a culture additional to their own is almost sure to have a collection of hilarious experiences dealing with mispronunciations or misunderstandings.

One thing that keeps amusing me is the language, and no matter how long I have been in this country, I find new situations where I am completely caught off guard, as I will illustrate further along. This particular aspect has been the source of lots of laughter and good memories among family and friends.

The stories I am including illustrate the way I interpreted a paragraph that I had read or a conversation I was having with someone.

I would say that artists are always hungry for information: ways to improve their exposure, new techniques to experiment with, new materials, etc. A few years ago, I found an article with good ideas on how to get accepted into art galleries.

I read the article and liked it a lot, but before I could start following the advice, I had to look for a word that I hadn't remembered hearing before. I was convinced that it definitely had to be a key for success. The paragraph read that I would have to write a "badass" résumé. Read it without a pause in between the words, with the accent on the last three letters. As you can imagine, this word was not in the dictionary . . . or Google as I researched. It was divided into two words.

I still could not find the relationship between something that sounded like some kind of swearing and writing a good résumé.

I hadn't been in the country too long. During a birthday party, the moment arrived when the cake had all the candles lit and the birthday person wasn't there. "Hurry up!" I said. "The sperm is going to fall all over the cake!" I was pulled aside quietly by my husband, who was wondering what exactly I wanted to say.

I told him *esperma* is the Spanish word for candle wax. I thought I would fudge it a bit, but I was obviously very wrong!

Many years ago, my ex-husband and I went to dinner with one of his longtime friends, who started telling stories from his childhood. He mentioned in one of his anecdotes how poor they were and how he and his friends would go to the butcher store to ask for "cold cat butts," which sounds normal for any American.

I didn't say anything right away, but I could not stop thinking about this strange story. I had been living in this country for a while and never heard of people eating cats. Finally, I could not keep quiet any longer and decided to ask: "Do people here in the States eat cats? Are the butts some kind of delicacy? And why have I never heard of this?"

Our friend could not stop laughing! He meant "cold cut butts," the ends separated from the cold cuts that are sliced for sale.

I have a dear friend named Fehmida who lives in Dallas. We met in Los Angeles at the laboratory where we both worked. She was just out of medical school at the time, and we have kept in touch all these years. Her husband plays classical guitar, and so does their son.

We were visiting them, and one of the activities she had planned and was very eager to tell me about was a violin concert with a very famous player, who would be playing "with his knees."

As I usually do on these occasions, I first pondered the situation in my mind. There was no way that someone could play the violin in such a strange way. I had to ask.

What she meant was that the violinist and his *niece* would be playing together. We still laugh about it every time we get together.

I have been known to replace some words with others of my own creation when I have to say something in a hurry or can't remember the proper word.

Weeds from the garden: "Plants that grow without permission."

When the bag of strawberries in the refrigerator was leaking: "Hurry up! I need a towel! The strawberries are leaving the bag!"

The strong rain left giant "poodles" on the street.

After Monica started going to school, she would mention words totally new to me since I didn't grow up in this country. The first time she told me that she was going to "hang" with some friends, I automatically went into "graphics mode" in my mind, and I imagined them hanging from a nail on a wall. I knew this wasn't the case, but it sounded very funny to me as a foreigner.

"Mom, we had a ball at the party!" I couldn't think of a reason for a ball at an indoors teen party. . . .

"HANGING OUT" (PENCIL DRAWING)

 FINALLY

So far, I have read two books about personal stories from young women who have been diagnosed with a terminal illness, in addition to the book *Being Mortal*, by Atul Gawande.

I feel immensely sad when a young person is given such news, especially if they have small children. I have had a good life in terms of doing the things I wanted. I am over sixty, and this news is probably not as devastating as it would be for a younger person. Still, I felt full of energy before I was diagnosed; I had many plans for the autumn of my life. No one wants to give that up.

People who suffer from cancer usually go through devastating treatments to stop the advance of the condition, and some will be lucky enough to experience encouraging results or at least periods of remission.

ALS patients have no chances and no treatments. So far, there are a couple of drugs that will prolong the life of the patient for around three months, I think. It is not easy to live unable to function on most levels. I have no desire to agree to a medication if there is not even a chance for a more positive outcome.

I sometimes read stories published on the newsletter sponsored by the ALS Association. Very frequently I read about people that have gotten the disorder and have turned things around helping thousands of others.

I wish I could have come up with some special idea to make a difference. The biggest financial help so far has come from the Ice Bucket Challenge, which collected much-needed funds for research and helped to spread awareness, since there is a big percentage of the population that has no knowledge of the disease or its devastating effects.

I also wish I had some meaningful advice to give others. I feel empty-handed. I applaud those who succeed in staying optimistic. I am working on it. I am making an effort to be mindful and enjoy each pleasure no matter how small. I am still trying to be a better person and endure what is happening with grace and valor.

I chose to write these essays because writing gives my soul a break. I wish I could do it in style, as I admire elegant prose myself, but we can give only what we have.

I came across an article written by Dudley Clendinen, a fine writer who also suffered from ALS. In an essay in *The New York Times*, titled "The Good Short Life," he illustrated in a more eloquent manner some thoughts and ideas I have expressed about this condition.

I also chose not to emphasize too much the deterioration that is so noticeable as time passes. I wanted to write from the point of view of an immigrant, about what it takes to arrive to another country on your own and how it affects the lives of those in the family.

I wanted to write especially about being an artist. Maybe if I had more time I would have written two or three separate books because there are many other stories.

As an artist, I have experienced a lot of satisfaction as well as disappointment—rejection is common. Yet I appreciate all the connections I was able to make and the pleasure derived from those. If you own one of my paintings, I hope that it is because it "called you." You felt invited to get closer and share its space, just like a company of a dear one. Every time you look at it, I want you to feel the presence of my soul, because all of me went into the making of each piece. I didn't paint to accumulate volume. Instead, the purpose was to tell a story hidden in plain sight, one painting at a time.

I have had plenty of good luck when it was important, and I have had the most supportive and dear friends and neighbors anyone could wish for, a loving daughter, a close-knit family, and a caring husband. I thank each of you from the bottom of my heart, even if I don't mention you by name.

I am especially happy and grateful that life has given me the tools to be able to paint. As a result, I have experienced many rewards, one of which has been being a member of a small group of artists that has been meeting regularly for about eighteen years. Each artist and friend has a special gift to give in terms of expertise and also comfort, especially during difficult times.

To the best of my abilities, I will continue to push my limits to squeeze in as much life as I can.

. . . One more thing:

Have you realized—and been grateful for—how amazing it is that you can walk? Cherish that simple fact every minute of your life.

"POSSIBILITIES" (ACRYLIC ON CANVAS)

AFTERWORD

A Conversation With
Author/Artist Patricia Riascos

On her upbringing in Colombia

I grew up in a relatively small town right in the middle of the coffee region in Colombia, surrounded by amazing landscapes and the most beautiful greenery—something that you truly appreciate once you have left it behind.

How travels have influenced her artwork

My art is, for the most part, emotional. When I travel or go back to Colombia, the feelings that I gather inspire me. As many people know, Colombia has suffered more than forty years of terrorism, but people like me, who are part of the diaspora, have not lived those difficult times. Several years ago, I spent a good amount of time reading and learning about this suffering, which inspired me to create a small series representing my sorrow as I learned the facts. I have not shown most of those paintings.

On quitting a career as a medical lab technologist to become an artist

The change to art happened slowly, coinciding with fewer hours at the laboratory. I feel great satisfaction being able to dedicate more time to something that makes the hours go by without me noticing and resolves the urge to create. The results are a source of happiness for me beyond any limits.

Her work in abstract art versus representational art

I have worked in the representational style but never too close to a complete copy of the subject. I have always admired abstract art but never actually had classes. I felt a great deal of curiosity about learning and decided that I would immerse myself in it. In my opinion, abstract art is a bit more difficult; there is nothing to copy from, and everything has to flow from your own intentions. It also demands a more disciplined sense of design, contrary to what people may believe. At the moment, I am mixing both elements.

Use of squares and structured shapes in paintings that are otherwise free flowing

I have actually thought a lot about this. There is the idea of a person who is a "square," who is supposed to be unwilling to accept other beliefs or external influences. However, I find that squares are very versatile in a painting: They add variation, texture, and fun, especially when mixed with a free-flowing style. For me, lines are also a very adaptable element. I enjoy using them. They can be very expressive, strong, or delicate. Picasso is my favorite artist. I have studied and admired how he could depict almost an entire painting with a few strokes. I use lines at all stages, sometimes as the final touches on wide spaces.

Paintings with written messages—what determines which get them

I enjoy writing. My mind is constantly at work as I go about my day. I collect all those thoughts in a little notebook. Sometimes, when I am deciding on my next project, I refer back to my notes. Then a painting is born and those words go on it, or it will be the title of the next painting. One of my favorite examples occurred after I was moving from a house that I had lived in for twenty-one years. During the time I spent packing, I started to think about how fortunate I was to have so much to pack and how the process was almost like reviewing your life and remembering the nice things that people have given to you. As a result, "Nothing like packing to move to see your life in front of your eyes" is written in one of my paintings.

Paintings that come easily versus those that don't

The fact that I could come up with what could be considered a successful painting is rewarding no matter what. If the painting went through a long process, it is like a child that demanded a lot of time and patience. Paintings are very much like children to me; it is very hard to let go of them. Once, I sold a very dear painting to an institution. On one occasion, I went to see how it looked "on location." When I saw it, I wanted to cry. It was hanging in a long, somewhat dark corridor, on a wall too big for its size. I felt that it was very lonely. I wanted to buy it back!

Advice she would give to her younger self

Work harder, invest more time when possible, and think well before you go into endeavors that look like great opportunities. Do better research and, more important, a better soul search.

(Adapted from an interview originally published in *American Lifestyle* magazine, December 2018.)

For more information, visit patriciariascosart.com.

About the Author

Patricia Riascos was born in Colombia and enjoys dual citizenship with the United States. She earned a bachelor of science degree in laboratory medical technology and worked in a stat (urgent testing) laboratory at the main facility of a large HMO in California. She went on to work in a Michigan laboratory as part of a team dedicated to helping patients with infertility issues.

It is art, however, that has always been in her heart, and she remained dedicated to making time to pursue her passion—eventually working her way toward a fine arts degree, first at California State University, Fullerton, and later at Wayne State University in Michigan.

In 2012 Riascos began to experience the symptoms of ALS, unbeknownst to her at the time. Though she is no longer able to walk, she still considers herself fortunate to have not experienced the loss of her voice, one of the first symptoms of the disease in most people. At the moment of this writing, she is still participating in all aspects of life as much as possible and also paints, just on a smaller scale.

Riascos lives with her husband, Harlan, in Michigan. Her daughter, Monica, has just relocated from Chicago to Detroit.